THE

IMPENDING CRISIS

OF

1860;

OR THE PRESENT CONNECTION OF THE

METHODIST EPISCOPAL CHURCH

WITH

SLAVERY,

AND OUR DUTY IN REGARD TO IT.

BY H. MATTISON,

OF THE BLACK RIVER CONFERENCE.

"This will be the last opportunity that God's true servants will ever have to restore the M. E. Church to her original character, and preserve her honor in the grandest moral conflict of the age."—*Correspondent.*

NEW YORK:

MASON BROTHERS, No. 46 WALKER STREET.

1859.

"We believe that Slavery has no more constitutional right in the Methodist Church than the Devil himself; and we are determined to use all befitting measures to drive it out."

REV. ABEL STEVENS, *in Zion's Herald for Sept.* 27, 1843.

HEAR, O ISRAEL!

"Hear, I pray you, ye chiefs of Jacob,
And ye princes of the house of Israel;
Is it not yours to know what is right?
Ye that hate good, and love evil;
Who tear their skin from off them,
And their flesh from off their bones;
Who devour the flesh of my people,
And flay from off them their skin;
And their bones they dash in pieces;
And chop them asunder, as morsels for the pot,
And as flesh thrown into the midst of the cauldron."

MICAH iii. 1–3.—*Lowth's Notes on Isaiah.*

TO ALL

MINISTERS AND PRIVATE MEMBERS

OF THE

METHODIST EPISCOPAL CHURCH,

WHO DESIRE TO

WALK IN THE OLD PATHS,

AND TO SEE OUR BELOVED ZION PURGED FROM THE

SIN AND DISGRACE OF SLAVEHOLDING,

THIS CONTRIBUTION

TO THE HOLY CAUSE OF "EXTIRPATION"

IS RESPECTFULLY DEDICATED,

BY THEIR FRIEND AND FELLOW-LABORER,

THE AUTHOR.

CONTENTS.

THE IMPENDING CRISIS.

CHAPTER I.

ORIGINAL POSITION OF METHODISM IN REGARD TO SLAVERY.

In this chapter we design to show that from 1739 to 1784, or during the first forty-five years of our denominational history, Methodism was *intensely anti-slavery*, both in theory and in practice—a society of *practical abolitionists*.*

I. John Wesley *was an earnest abolitionist.*

1. The "*General Rules of the United Society*" were written by Mr. Wesley, May 1, 1743. (*Works*, vol. v. p. 190.) These rules forbid "doing harm," "doing to others as we would not they should do to us," "doing what we know is not for the glory of God," &c. Now, unless there is "no harm" in holding a fellow-being as a slave, and it is in accordance with the golden rule, and "for the glory of God," it is certain that these rules forbade all slaveholding; and, if honestly executed, would cut it up root and branch. These are the Rules now found in our Discipline, page 25 and onward.

2. In 1774 Mr. Wesley first published his "*Thoughts upon Slavery*," in tract form. The whole drift of the tract is not only against the slave-trade, but against every species of slaveholding. He says:

---

* We use the term "abolitionist" in its true philological sense, as meaning "a person who favors abolition, or the immediate emancipation of slaves." The false meanings attached to the word by slaveholders, in order to cast odium upon the anti-slavery cause, is no reason why we should accept it as a synonym for fanaticism and infidelity. The time has gone by when a man can be a real anti-slavery man and not be an abolitionist; and if any one is not willing to be called an abolitionist, he should never profess to be anti-slavery.

"But waiving, for the present, all other considerations, I strike at the root of this complicated villany: I absolutely deny all slaveholding to be consistent with any degree of natural justice."—(*Works*, vol. vi. p. 286.)

On the next page he says, "all slavery is as irreconcilable to justice as to mercy"—is "utterly inconsistent with mercy," &c.; and in replying to the plea that slavery was *necessary* in order to the cultivation of the soil, he says:

"I deny that villany is ever necessary. It is impossible that it should ever be necessary for any reasonable creature to violate all the laws of justice, mercy, and truth. No circumstances can make it necessary for a man to burst in sunder all the ties of humanity. It can never be necessary for a rational being to sink himself below a brute. A man can be under no necessity of degrading himself into a wolf."—(Pages 287, 288.)

On page 292, he declares that "men-buyers are exactly on a level with men-stealers," and thus vehemently exhorts the slaveholder:

"'The blood of thy brother' (for, whether thou wilt believe it or no, such he is in the sight of Him that made him), 'crieth against thee from the earth,' from the ship, and from the water. Oh! whatever it costs, put a stop to its cry before it be too late; instantly, at any price, were it the half of your goods, deliver thyself from blood-guiltiness! Thy hands, thy bed, thy furniture, thy house, thy lands, are at present stained with blood. Surely it is enough: accumulate no more guilt; spill no more the blood of the innocent! Do not hire another to shed blood; do not pay him for doing it! Whether you are a Christian or no, show yourself a man! Be not more savage than a lion or a bear!"

Next he anticipates and refutes the false reasoning of the slaveholder as follows:

"Perhaps you will say, 'I do not buy any negroes; I only use those left me by my father.' So far is well; but is it enough to satisfy your own conscience? Had your father, have you, has any man living, a right to use another as a slave? It cannot be, even setting Revelation aside. It cannot be that either war or contract can give any man such a property in another as he has in his sheep and oxen. Much less is it possible that any child of man should ever be born a slave. Liberty is the right of every human creature, as soon as he breathes the vital air; and no human law can deprive him of that right which he derives from the law of nature.

"If, therefore, you have any regard to justice (to say nothing of mercy, nor the revealed law of God), render unto all their due. Give liberty to whom liberty is due; that is, to every child of man, to every partaker of human nature. Let none serve you but by his own act and deed, by his own voluntary choice. Away with all whips, all chains, all compulsion! Be gentle towards all men; and see that you invariably do unto every one as you would he should do unto you."

Finally, the tract closes with the following prayer:

"O thou God of love! thou who art loving to every man, and whose mercy is over all thy works; thou who art the Father of the spirits of all flesh, and who art rich in mercy unto all; thou who hast mingled of one blood all the nations upon earth; have compassion upon these outcasts of men, who are trodden down as dung upon the earth! Arise, and help these that have no helper, whose blood is spilt upon the ground like water! Are not these also the work of thine own hands, the purchase of thy Son's blood? Stir them up to cry unto thee in the land of their captivity; and let their complaint come up before thee; let it enter into thy ears!"

How does such language comport with the sensitiveness of some of our modern Methodists, even on free soil, who are offended if the slave is even remembered at the throne of grace in the house of God? Have they the spirit as well as the name of Methodists? Could they have endured the abolitionism of JOHN WESLEY? Indeed, would he, if now alive, be tolerated in more than one half of the pulpits of American Methodism? We doubt if he would, but let the reader judge.

3. Mr. Wesley frequently corresponded with WILBERFORCE and CLARKSON, the great leaders in the movement for the abolition of slavery in the West Indies, and cheered them on in their difficult and arduous undertaking.

In 1787, when the Abolition Committee was formed, Mr. Wesley wrote them an encouraging letter. The following account of its contents is taken from CLARKSON'S *History of the Abolition of the Slave-Trade*, vol. i. p. 447:

"Mr. Wesley, whose letter was read next, informed the committee of the great satisfaction which he also had experienced when he heard of their formation. He conceived that their design, while it would destroy the slave-trade, would also strike at the root of the shocking abomination of slavery. He desired to forewarn them that they must expect difficulties and great opposition from those who were interested in the system; that these were a powerful body; and that they would raise all their forces when they perceived their craft to be in danger. They would employ hireling writers, who would have neither justice nor mercy. But the committee were not to be dismayed by such treatment, nor even if some of those who professed good-will towards them should turn against them. As to himself, he would do all he could to promote the object of their institution," &c.

On the 30th of October, 1787, a second letter from Mr. Wesley was read before the committee, stating that he had read the publication which the committee had sent him, and took, if possible, a still deeper interest in their cause.—(*Works*, vol. vii. p. 238.)

On the 26th of February, 1791, Mr. Wesley addressed the following to Mr. Wilberforce:

"LONDON, *February* 26, 1791.

"DEAR SIR,—Unless the divine power has raised you up to be as *Athanasius contra mundum*, I see not how you can go through your glorious enterprise, in opposing that execrable villany, which is the scandal of religion, of England, and of human nature. Unless God has raised you up for this very thing, you will be worn out by the opposition of men and devils. But, 'if God be for you, who can be against you?' Are all of them together stronger than God? Oh, 'be not weary in well-doing!' Go on, in the name of God and in the power of his might, till even American slavery (the vilest that ever saw the sun) shall vanish away before it.

"Reading this morning a tract, written by a poor African, I was particularly struck by that circumstance—that a man who has a black skin, being wronged or outraged by a white man, can have no redress; it being a law, in all our colonies, that the oath of a black against a white goes for nothing. What villany is this!

"That He who has guided you from your youth up may continue to strengthen you in this and all things, is the prayer of, dear sir, your affectionate servant, JOHN WESLEY."*

Mr. Wesley died March 2, 1791; so that the above letter was written *only four days before his departure from time!*

In an anti-slavery speech made in City-Road Chapel, some forty years after Mr. Wesley's death, Mr. Watson said:

"We stand near the grave of a man who was one of the first to lift up his voice against West India bondage, and to plead the wrongs of Africa, with an eloquence which is at once touching from its pathos, and irresistible from its power.† Were that voice now living, it would give its sanction to our efforts; and in this place, where that voice has been so often heard, we may feel that 'though dead,' on this subject especially 'he yet speaketh.' "—(JACKSON'S *Life of Watson*, p. 377.)

Thus, from first to last, both by word and deed and pen, did JOHN WESLEY proclaim himself an earnest and uncompromising CHRISTIAN ABOLITIONIST.

II. *The early Methodists generally, both preachers and people, were all abolitionists.*

"The preachers entered fully into his [Mr. Wesley's] views; and probably it [the tract on slavery] had no small influence in stimulating the natural ardor of Dr. Coke against slavery in his first visit to America."‡ So thoroughly did they, one and all, take hold of the matter of emancipation in the West Indies, at a subsequent period, that more petitions were sent into Parliament from the Wesleyan Methodists alone, than

---

* See *Works*, vol. vii. p. 237; also *Life of Wilberforce by his Son.*

† Alluding to Mr. Wesley's able and stirring tract against slavery; and the very strong views on this subject, which that eminent man was known to entertain.—DR. JACKSON.

‡ *British Methodism and Slavery*, by Rev. W. J. Shrewsbury, England, in Methodist Quarterly Review, for April, 1858, p. 187.

from all other Non-conformist bodies put together. The account stands thus:

	Petitions.	Signatures.
Wesleyan Methodists................................	1,953	229,426
Presented from twenty-one other Dissenting bodies,....	923	122,978
Excess of Wesleyans over all other Dissenters.......	1,030	106,448

There were also presented from other sources, 2194 petitions, containing 957,527 signatures; making a grand total of 5071 petitions, and 1,309,931 signatures. This flood of petitions coming up *from the people*, and inundating Parliament, was the immediate cause of the abolition of slavery in the West Indies.* And none were so conspicuous in collecting and presenting them, as were the followers of the then departed JOHN WESLEY,—the numbers just quoted fully evincing their earnestness in the cause of abolition.†

III. RICHARD WATSON, *the great systematic theologian of Methodism, was an abolitionist.*

In his *Theological Institutes*, which is a text-book in which every Methodist preacher is examined before his admission into Conference, he shows slaveholding to be utterly irreconcilable with Christianity. The argument is too long to quote, but we refer to it as explicit and incontrovertible.‡

In a speech made by him in Exeter Hall, London, April 23, 1831, he said:

"It has been said that Christian instruction should be employed, in order to *prepare the slaves for the enjoyment of freedom*, after some very long period has elapsed. Now, in his [Mr. Watson's] opinion, *it was impossible to spread Christianity through the mass of the slave population so long as it continues in slavery.* Christianity had indeed had some noble triumphs in the West Indies, but few, comparatively, among field negroes; and this was the great objection to the system. Legislators might give them Sabbaths, but they would be robbed of them practically, for there was a power in every planter greater than the power of the British government itself. Christian zeal might multiply missionaries, and yet none of these missionaries could enter an estate without leave from the owner to instruct his slaves; the consequence was, that a variety of obstacles were continually thrown in the way of the diffusion of Christianity throughout the population at large. But even if it were possible to ex-

* And this is our main hope of ever influencing the General Conference to free the Methodist Episcopal Church from slavery. *The people* are mighty, under God, to the pulling down of strong-holds.

† Ibid. p. 205.

‡ See *Institutes*, part iii. chap. iv.

tend Christianity throughout the mass of the population, those persons who imagined that it would make the slaves quiet and content with slavery were greatly mistaken. [Hear, hear.] Christianity would make better *servants*, but worse *slaves*. It creates honesty, industry, and conscientiousness; but it cannot create them without the love of freedom. Slavery was felt to be an evil most deeply by the man who had been brought under the influence of Christianity. [Cheers.] By religion the mind becomes enlightened, the sensibilities acute and tender, and the social relations more united and strengthened. Would a Christian father then endure it as well as a Pagan father, that his children should be separated from him; that his daughters, whom he had educated in virtue, should be subdued for pollution by the influence of the whip, a thing most general throughout the slave colonies; and if the whip made the instrument of defending such an outrage? Our religion was not a religion to teach slaves to kiss their chains, but a religion to teach freemen how to use their freedom."—(*London Anti-Slavery Reporter*, vol. iv. p. 227.)

In the fall of 1834, the British Anti-Slavery Society published its first report. Dr. Bunting was a member of the society, and on reading this first report, "Mr. Watson's fears concerning it vanished;" and in an article which he wrote for the Wesleyan Magazine, he pronounced it a "truly patriotic and Christian society," with which none should hesitate to co-operate. (See *Life of Jackson*, p. 292.) Further on, his biographer says:

"In the righteous and benevolent feelings of the abolitionists, Mr. Watson strongly participated, and cheerfully lent all the assistance in his power to further the desirable object which they all have in view."—(*Ibid.* p. 372.)

At the Leeds Conference in 1830, Mr. Watson "thought that the time was come when the Methodist Conference ought, more publicly and distinctly, to bear its testimony against slavery, as existing in the British colonies." Accordingly he drew up a series of the most thorough and practical abolition resolutions, which were adopted by the Conference. Take the following as a sample:

"*Resolved*, That, as a body of Christian ministers, we feel ourselves called upon again to record our solemn judgment, that the holding of human beings in a state of slavery is in direct opposition to all the principles of natural right, and to the benign spirit of the religion of Christ."

The resolutions then proceed to portray the evils of slavery—its effects upon the marriage institution, &c., and to exhort the members of the societies to unite with others in signing and circulating petitions "for its speedy and universal abolition." Still further, the resolutions advised all Methodist voters to "give their influence and votes only to those candidates who pledged themselves to support, in Parliament, the most effectual measures for the entire abolition of slavery throughout the colonies of the British empire."—(*Life*, pp. 374, 375.)

In accordance with the spirit of his resolutions, Mr. Watson canvassed his circuit for signers to petitions; held meetings on week-day evenings, and made abolition speeches, and was as zealous and persevering as any of our American "agitators" have ever been.—(*Ibid.* p. 377.)

In one of these meetings, held in City-Road Chapel in 1830, Mr. Watson made one of these abolition speeches. It may be found at full length in his Life by Jackson, pp. 377–383, and reminds us forcibly of the speech of Dr. Thomson, at the last General Conference. It goes over the whole ground; takes up "the reasons that have been lately put forth by the pro-slavery party," as he calls them; answers the Scripture argument; and cuts up the whole vile upas of slavery, root and branch. A stronger abolition speech is scarcely to be found in the English language; and no man could now circulate it among our Methodists in Maryland and Virginia, without being tarred and feathered, if not hung outright. So we garnish the sepulchres of the prophets who have passed away, and yet persecute them in the person of their uncorrupted successors.

IV. Dr. Adam Clarke, *the great Methodist commentator, was an abolitionist.*

In his comment on Isa. lviii. 6, he says:

> "How can any nation pretend to fast or worship God at all, or dare to profess that they believe in the existence of such a being, while they carry on the *slave-trade*, and traffic in the souls, blood, and bodies of men! Oh, ye most flagitious of knaves, and worst of hypocrites, cast off at once the mask of religion; and deepen not your endless perdition by professing the *faith* of our *Lord Jesus Christ*, while ye continue in this traffic."

At the close of his notes on 1 Cor., chapter vii., he says:

> "And, to conclude, I here register my testimony against the unprincipled, inhuman, anti-Christian, and diabolical *slave-trade*, with all its *authors*, *promoters*, *abettors*, *and sacrilegious gains;* as well as against the great devil, the father of it and them."

It is somewhat strange that such sentiments have never indicted Clarke's Commentary in the South, as an "incendiary document."

V. REV. JOSEPH BRADBURN, *one of the most noted of the early Wesleyan preachers, was an abolitionist.*

Writing to the Northern Independent, May, 1858, Rev. J. D. Long says:

"I have recently discovered in the great Philadelphia Library, an old tract on slavery of about sixteen pages, printed in London by that celebrated Methodist preacher, Joseph Bradburn. I consider it a far stronger production, both in argument and comprehensiveness, than Wesley's tract on the same subject. We think that some wealthy anti-slavery Methodist could not do a better thing than to have it reprinted and scattered broadcast over the Church." [We have since received a transcript of this Tract.]

VI. DR. THOMAS COKE, *the first Bishop of the Methodist Episcopal Church, was an abolitionist.*

In proof of this declaration, take the following from his biography. Speaking of his labors in Virginia in 1785, Mr. Drew says:

"Hitherto, while Dr. Coke had preserved a profound silence on the subject of negro slavery, all were pleased, and he was permitted to go on his way in peace. But no sooner did he lift up his voice against the injustice of the traffic, than it became a signal for the commencement of hostilities against him. In the province of Virginia, while preaching in a barn, on Sunday the 9th of April, 1785, he took occasion to introduce the subject of slavery, and expatiate on its injustice in terms that were not calculated to flatter his auditors."—(*Life by Samuel Drew, old octavo edition*, p. 133.)

The result, of course, was angry tumult among the slaveholders, and violent persecution. A lady offered fifty pounds to any one who would give the preacher fifty lashes. But he escaped unhurt. And, speaking of the effect of the sermon, his biographer says:

"But rage and hostility were not the only effects produced by this discourse. The magistrate who had espoused the cause of Dr. Coke began to view the subject in a more serious light, and, to show that he acted from a pure principle, immediately emancipated fifteen slaves. The report of his conduct extended the benefit still further, and induced another to follow so laudable an example, and to emancipate eight slaves. And the united examples of both induced another to emancipate one. These effects were instantaneously visible; but to what extent his faithful but sharp reproofs operated in secret, we must not expect fully to know until we enter the world of spirits."—(*Ibid.* pp. 133, 134.)

About this time, Dr. Coke drew up a petition to the legislature of North Carolina, praying them to pass an act, that, "in a land which boasted of independence, the slaveholders might at least be permitted to emancipate their slaves." This petition was signed by Coke and Asbury, and by the whole

Conference of Primitive Methodist preachers. They were all abolitionists in those better days of our history.—(*Ibid.* pp. 134, 135.)

The biography proceeds:

"On repairing from North Carolina to the State of Virginia, in which the law permits the emancipation of slaves, Dr. Coke again appealed to the dealers in human flesh and blood," &c.

And so he continued to do for some time after. In company with Mr. Asbury, he visited General Washington, then President of the United States, at Mount Vernon, and requested him to sign their petition. This he declined to do, on the ground that he was a citizen of Virginia, and ought not to petition the Legislature of North Carolina; but at the same time avowed his hearty approval of the principles of the petition.—(*Ibid.* pp. 135, 136.)

On returning from the West Indies to Charleston, S. C., in February, 1787, it is said of him, that—

"During his former visit to the continent, Dr. Coke had frequently lifted his voice against the slavery which was tolerated in the United States. This had exposed him to many perils. To some of these his eyes were fully open, but in several instances his danger lay concealed. The arm of legal power had been lifted against him; by a furious mob he had been secretly pursued, and a bullet of an assassin, who couched in ambush to take away his life, had been levelled at him. * * * * He was now informed, while passing through the country, that, from the spirited manner in which he had opposed this sanctioned enormity when on his former visit, the slaveholders had been so exasperated as to present a bill against him to the grand-jury. This bill was found; and although he had left the country at that time, no less than ninety persons engaged to pursue the fugitive and bring him back to colonial justice."—(*Life*, pp. 180, 181.)

Further on we are told that one man armed himself with a gun, and actually followed Dr. Coke with a fixed determination to take away his life. One ground of this violent opposition was, that Dr. Coke had originated the petition to the legislature of North Carolina for a law allowing the emancipation of slaves.—(*Life*, p. 182.)

VII. Francis Asbury, *the second Bishop of the Methodist Episcopal Church, was an abolitionist.*

In proof of this, take the following extracts from his journals, under the dates affixed to the several paragraphs:

"1776.—After preaching at the Point, I met the class, and then the black people, some of whose unhappy masters forbid their coming for religious instruction. How will the sons of oppression answer for their conduct, when the great Proprietor of all shall call them to account!"—(Vol. i. p. 289.)

"1780.—Spoke to some select friends about slavekeeping, but they could not bear it. This I know—God will plead the cause of the oppressed, though it gives offence to say so here. O Lord, banish the INFERNAL SPIRIT OF SLAVERY from thy dear Zion!

"Lord, help thy people! There are many things which are painful to me, but cannot yet be removed, especially slavekeeping and its attendant circumstances. The Lord will certainly hear the cries of the oppressed, *naked*, *starving* creatures. O my God! think on this land. *Amen.*"—(*Ibid.* p. 293.)

"1783.—We all agreed (at the Virginia Conference) in the spirit of African liberty, and strong testimonies were borne in its favor at our love-feast."—(*Ibid.* p. 356.)

"1785.—At the Virginia Conference," he says, "I found the minds of the people greatly agitated with our rules against slavery, and a proposed petition to the General Assembly for the emancipation of the blacks. Colonel —— and Dr. Coke disputed on the subject, and the colonel used some threats. Next day, brother O. Kelly let fly at them, and they were made angry enough; we, however, came off with whole bones."—(*Ibid.* p. 384.)

"We waited on General Washington, who received us very politely, and gave us his opinion against slavery."—(*Ibid.* p. 385.)

"1788.—*Virginia.* Other persuasions are less supine, and their ministers boldly preach against the freedom of slaves. Our brother Everett, with no less zeal and boldness, cries aloud for liberty and emancipation."

"1798.—My mind is much pained. Oh, to be dependent on slaveholders is, in part, to be a slave, and I was free born! I am brought to conclude that slavery will exist in Virginia perhaps for ages; there is not *a sufficient sense of religion nor liberty to* DESTROY *it.* I judge, in after ages, it will be so that poor men and free men will not live among slaveholders, but will go to new lands; they only who are concerned in and dependent on them, will stay in old Virginia.

"On Saturday, I had a close conversation with some of our local ministry. We were happy to find seven out of ten were not in the spirit or practice of slavery.

"I assisted Philip Sands to draw up an agreement for our officiary to sign, against slavery. Thus we may know the real sentiments of our local preachers. It appears to me, *that we can never fully reform the people, until we reform the preachers*—and that hitherto, except purging the travelling connection, we have been working at the wrong end. But, if it be lawful for local preachers to hold slaves, then it is lawful for travelling preachers also, and they may keep plantations and overseers upon their quarters; but this *reproach of inconsistency must be rolled away.*"

"*South Carolina*, 1801.—A Solomon Reeves let me know that he had seen the Address* signed by me, and was quite confident there were no arguments to prove that slavery was repugnant to the spirit of the Gospel! What absurdities will not men defend! If the Gospel will tolerate slavery, what will it not authorize? I am strangely mistaken if this said Mr. Reeves has more grace than is necessary, or more of Solomon than the name."—(*Ibid.* p. 15.)

"Joseph Ballard and his wife are gone to rest. John Perry, a pious soul, is also gone to his reward. Neither he nor Ballard were slaveholders. Hail, happy souls!"—(*Ibid.* p. 18.)

---

* This is doubtless the petition drawn up by Dr. Coke, mentioned on page 12.

"1810.—We have hard labor and suffering. I do not dare to complain, when I see the wretched fate of the poor Africans in slavery."—(*Ibid.* p. 300.)

"1814.—*Georgia.* Away with the false cant, that the better you use the negroes, the worse they will use you! Make them good; then teach them the fear of God, and learn to fear him yourselves, ye masters! I understand not the doctrine of cruelty. As soon as the poor Africans see me, they spring with life to the boat, and make a heavy flat skim along like a light canoe. Poor, starved souls—God will judge!"—(*Ibid.* p. 376.)

In a pamphlet, attributed by Mr. Flournoy, of Georgia, to Rev. Gabriel Capers, brother of Bishop Capers, we have the following:

"Many years ago," says Mr. C., "the venerable Bishops Coke and Asbury published a pamphlet on slavery, which compelled the enlightened and benevolent legislature of South Carolina to pass an act authorizing any person to repair to Methodist meetings and disperse the negroes, whether assembled with or without permission from their owners. The act was justified by the first law of nature, self-defence, and based upon the fact that Methodism at that *period*, whether at the North or South, was identified with the most DEADLY OPPOSITION TO SLAVERY. It continued in force, and with the utmost propriety, too, until the ministers of that denomination CEASED *to assail the institution of bondage*, and to expel the members of their societies for buying and selling a slave under any circumstances."

VIII. FREEBORN GARRETTSON, *one of the first Methodist preachers in this country, and a companion of Asbury, was a practical abolitionist.*

Mr. Garrettson was once a slaveholder himself; and while such, thought he had experienced religion. At times he was exceedingly happy, and again, to use his own words, his mind would be "encompassed with darkness and the most severe distress." After one of these struggles, during a part of which he had lain with his face to the ground, he says:

"I arose from the earth, and advancing towards the house in deep thought, I came to this conclusion, that I would exclude myself from the the society of men, and live in a cell upon bread and water, mourning out my days for having grieved my Lord. I went into my room and sat in one position till nine o'clock. I then threw myself on the bed, and slept till morning. Although it was the Lord's day, I did not intend to go to any place of worship; neither did I desire to see any person, but wished to pass my time away in total solitude. I continued reading the Bible till eight, and then, under a sense of duty, called the family together for prayer. As I stood with a book in my hand, in the act of giving out a hymn, this thought powerfully struck my mind—'It is not right for you to keep your fellow-creatures in bondage; you must let the oppressed go free.' I knew it was that same blessed voice which had spoken to me before—till then, I had never suspected that the practice of slave-keeping was wrong; I had not read a book on the subject, nor been told so by any—I paused a minute, and then replied, 'Lord, the oppressed shall go free.' And I was as clear of them in my mind, as if I had never owned one. I told them they did not belong to me, and that I did not desire their services without making them a compensation: I was now at liberty to proceed in worship. After singing, I kneeled to pray. Had I the tongue of an angel, I could not fully describe what I felt: all my dejection, and that melancholy gloom which preyed upon me, vanished in a moment; a divine sweetness ran through my whole frame. It was God, not man, that taught me the impropriety of holding slaves: and I shall never be able to praise him enough for it. My very heart has bled, since that, for slaveholders, especially those who make a profession of religion; for I believe it to be a crying sin."—(*Life of Garrettson, by* DR. BANGS, p. 39.)

Mr. Garrettson had not at this time united with the Methodist Societies, nor even attended a class-meeting; so that his convictions of duty as to his slaves, were not the result of any thing he had heard from any of their preachers. As he says, "it was God and not man who taught him the impropriety of holding slaves." And so God would teach every slaveholder, if he would listen either to the voice of conscience or of the Holy Scriptures. Both alike would say to him, "let the oppressed go free."

In a manuscript note found in his printed Journals after his departure, alluding to the above event, and written not long before his death, Mr. Garrettson says:

"I have since clearly seen the goodness of God in preparing me for future usefulness: I was a babe, and knew very little of the insinuations of our powerful foe. I shall always have an aversion to the practice of holding our fellow-creatures in abject slavery. It was the blessed God that taught me the rights of man."—(*Life*, pp. 39, 40.)

Of the sentiments of Bishop Whatcoat upon the subject of slavery we have no knowledge, beyond the strong presumption that he agreed with his fellow-laborers of that period; otherwise he would never have been elected bishop.

IX. WILLIAM MCKENDREE, *the fourth Bishop of the Methodist Episcopal Church, was also an abolitionist.*

Rev. F. S. DE HASS has recently brought to light an old document, dated 1806, and signed by Mr. McKendree. It is entitled "*An Address from the Quarterly Meeting Conference, in Livingston Circuit, to the Bishops and Members of the Western Conference;*" and contains the following:

* * * * "Though we cannot assist you with money at present to extend the work of the Lord, we can, no doubt, gladden your hearts by giving you a view of our purifying work at home. Isaiah saith, 'Undo the heavy burdens—let the oppressed go free—break every yoke—and thou shalt be like a watered garden—a spring of water, which faileth not; yea, thou shalt be the restorer of the paths to walk in.' This day our official breth-

ren voluntarily submitted all their slaves to the judgment of Conference, whether bought with their money before or after joining society, given, or born in their house. And we thereby had the unspeakable pleasure of decreeing salvation from slavery in favor of twenty-two immortal souls; we did not reprobate one of them. Now if the grace of God can prompt men to act thus, you may rest assured, that the God of grace never designed one immortal soul for eternal burnings.

"Brother Wm. Cude made a free offering of thirteen. Now eight of these cost him $1770, bought before he joined; the other five were given, or born in his house. Brother Josiah Ramsey offered up six on the altar of love; two of these cost him $850, the rest were born in his house. Brother James T. White, one living man, which was his all. Brothers Lewis Barker and Robert Galloway one apiece. All these are to have salvation recorded speedily. And Brother Thomas Randolph proposed his for the next quarterly meeting. When this is done, we shall, as far as we know, be free from the stain of blood in our official department. Glory, hallelujah! Praise ye the Lord!

"One thought more. If it is consistent with your authority, and it seemeth good unto you, we should be glad of liberty to exclude buying and selling from our Church, and to require of all slaveholders, who may hereafter become members of the Church, to submit their slaves to the judgment of Conference; who shall determine the time of servitude upon the same principle, and have a bill of manumission recorded in the same manner as the form of discipline requires in buying a slave.

"We are, dear fathers, your sons and fellow-laborers in the kingdom of Christ. "Signed in behalf and by order of Conference,

W. McKendree,
Jas. T. White."

This was only two years before Mr. McKendree's election to the episcopacy; and it proves most conclusively that, unless he fell from grace on this subject in the short space of two years, he was, at the time of his election to the episcopacy, a thorough-going extirpationist.

X. *The first Methodist preachers in America were almost to a man abolitionists.*

This is evident, not only from their general conduct in regard to slaveholding in the Church, but also from the action had in the several Conferences from 1780 to 1784 and onward. At the Conference held in Baltimore, in April, 1780, the following minute was adopted:

"*Quest.* 17. Does this Conference acknowledge that slavery is contrary to the laws of God, man, and nature, and hurtful to society; contrary to the dictates of conscience and pure religion, and doing that we would not others should do to us and ours? Do we pass our disapprobation on all our friends who keep slaves, and advise their freedom?

"*Ans.* Yes."—(*Bound Minutes*, vol. i. p. 12.)

This Conference, let it be remembered, was composed of all the Methodist preachers then in America—only twenty-four in all—and such was their noble testimony against slavery, even in the midst of it, and in the very slave-mart of Maryland. What a contrast with the resolutions passed, in the same city, seventy-seven years afterwards, namely, by the Baltimore Conference, in 1857. (See page 38.)

In 1783 we have the following rule:

"*Quest.* 10. What shall be done with our local preachers who hold slaves, contrary to the laws which authorize their freedom in any of the United States?

"We will try them another year. In the mean time, let every assistant [*i. e.* preacher] deal faithfully and plainly with every one, and report to the next Conference. It may then be necessary to suspend them."—(*Minutes*, vol. i. p. 18.)

The next year, May, 1784, we have the following:

"*Quest.* 12. What shall we do with our friends that will buy and sell slaves?

"*Ans.* If they buy with no other design than to hold them as slaves, and have been previously warned, they shall be expelled, and permitted to sell on no consideration.

"*Quest.* 13. What shall we do with our local preachers who will not emancipate their slaves, in the States where the laws admit of it?

"*Ans.* Try those in Virginia another year, and suspend the preachers in Maryland, Delaware, Pennsylvania, and New Jersey."—(*Minutes*, vol. i. p. 20.)

How much these resolves contributed towards the final abolition of slavery in the latter two States, who can tell? But the first question and answer shows most conclusively what the same body of men meant the next year, when they adopted and put into the Discipline* what is now known as the General Rule on Slavery. It was not the "*buying*" in itself that was forbidden, but the "*holding* them as slaves."

At the same Conference they ask:

"*Quest.* 22. What shall be done with our travelling preachers† that now are, or hereafter shall be, possessed of slaves, and refuse to manumit them where the law permits?

"*Ans.* Employ them no more."—(*Ibid.* p. 21.)

The same year, viz., on Christmas day, 1784, the Conference met in Philadelphia, and organized the Methodist Episcopal Church. At this Conference they prepared the first edition of the Discipline, and incorporated into it the most stringent rules for the extirpation of slavery from the Society. Among

---

* This first edition was published in Philadelphia in 1785.—(*Emory's Hist.* p. 80.)

† Here, for the first time, we have evidence that the deadly leprosy had fastened upon some of the ministry, probably through their marriage connections.

others, they added the following to Mr. Wesley's General Rules; thus forbidding—

"*The buying or selling of the bodies and souls of men, women, or children, with an intention to enslave them.*"

It is found in *italics* from the first, thus indicating its special importance in the eyes of those who inserted it.

Dr. Emory (*History of the Discipline*, p. 181) gives this new rule as first inserted in 1789; but Dr. Bangs (*Hist.* vol. i. pp. 213, 175) inserts it as put into the Discipline, in 1784.

This fact goes far to determine its real design and meaning. Only eight months before the same men had said, "If they buy with no other design than to hold them as slaves, and have been previously warned, they shall be expelled," &c.; and now, in embodying their views in a permanent discipline, they forbid "the buying or selling the bodies and souls of men, women, or children, with an intention to enslave them." How preposterous, therefore, to affirm, as Dr. Stevens and some others do, that the General Rule against slavery was only designed to prohibit *the traffic*, while it *tolerated*, and now even *protects* the *holding!* The truth is, it did not forbid the buying of slaves at all, provided the buyer wished to free them. It was plainly the *holding* of slaves against which the Rule was mainly levelled; and at the *selling*, only because it necessarily implied the right of property in man, and looked towards perpetual bondage. This is evident from the fact that in another part of this first Discipline we find the following:

"*Quest.* 43. What shall be done with those who buy or sell slaves, OR GIVE THEM AWAY?*

"*Ans.* They are immediately to be expelled, unless they buy them on purpose to free them."—(*Emory's Hist.* p. 44.)

And yet, in the face of all these facts—the known abolition principles of the preachers of that Conference; their previous efforts against slavery; their concurrent action in other parts of the Discipline, and especially the above—Dr. Stevens tells us that instead of the Rules forbidding slaveholding, it actually protects it, and even allows the giving away of slaves. Here are some of his expressions:

"The existing General Rule prohibits only the buying and selling, * * it implies the *right* to hold them by inheritance, * * slaveholding

* These capitals are our own.

itself is allowed by the General Rules, the organic law of the Church, * * the transmission of slaves in families was not intended to be prohibited," &c.—(*See speech at the last General Conference.*)

How different from his New England view of the Rule:

"We believe that slavery has no more constitutional right in the Methodist Church than the devil himself," &c.—(*Zion's Herald*, Sept. 27, 1843.)

But we must not be drawn too far aside from our main object. At this same Conference (1784), when the Methodist Episcopal Church was organized, and the first Discipline compiled, the following most thorough enactments were passed, outside of the General Rules, for the purifying of the infant Church from the deadly leaven of slavery:

"*Quest.* 42. What methods can we take to extirpate slavery?

"*Ans.* We are deeply conscious of the impropriety of making new terms of communion for a religious society already established, excepting on the most pressing occasion; and such we esteem the practice of holding our fellow-creatures in slavery. We view it as contrary to the golden law of God, on which hang all the law and the prophets, and the inalienable rights of mankind, as well as every principle of the revolution, to hold in the deepest debasement, in a more abject slavery than is, perhaps, to be found in any part of the world, except America, so many souls that are all capable of the image of God.

"We therefore think it our most bounden duty to take immediately some effectual method to extirpate this abomination from among us; and for this purpose we add the following to the rules of our societies, viz.:

"1. Every member of our society, who has slaves in his possession, shall, within twelve months after notice given to him by the assistant [*i. e.* preacher in charge], (which notice the assistants are required immediately, and without any delay, to give to their respective circuits), legally execute and record an instrument, whereby he emancipates and sets free every slave in his possession, who is between the ages of forty and forty-five, immediately; or, at farthest, when they arrive at the age of forty-five.

"And every slave who is between the ages of twenty-five and forty, immediately; or, at farthest, at the expiration of five years from the date of said instrument.

"And every slave who is between the ages of twenty and twenty-five, immediately; or, at farthest, when they arrive at the age of thirty.

"And every slave under the age of twenty, as soon as they arrive at the age of twenty-five at farthest.

"And every infant born in slavery, after the above-mentioned rules are complied with, immediately on its birth.

"2. Every assistant shall keep a journal, in which he shall regularly minute down the names and ages of all the slaves belonging to all the masters in his respective circuit, and also the date of every instrument executed and recorded for the manumission of the slaves, with the name of the court, book, and folio in which the said instruments respectively shall have been recorded; which journal shall be handed down in each circuit to the succeeding assistants.

"3. In consideration that these rules form a new term of communion, every person concerned, who will not comply with them, shall have liberty quietly to withdraw himself from our society, within the twelve months succeeding the notice given as aforesaid, otherwise the assistant shall exclude him in the society.

"No person so voluntarily withdrawn, or so excluded, shall ever partake of the Supper of the Lord with the Methodists, till he complies with the above requisitions.

"No person holding slaves shall, in future, be admitted into society, or to the Lord's Supper, till he previously complies with these rules concerning slavery.

"N. B. These rules are to affect the members of our society no further than as they are consistent with the laws of the States in which they reside.

"And respecting our brethren in Virginia that are concerned, and after due consideration of their peculiar circumstances, we allow them two years from the notice given, to consider the expediency of compliance or non-compliance with these rules.

"*Quest.* 43. What shall be done with those who buy or sell slaves, or give them away?

"*Ans.* They are immediately to be expelled, unless they buy them on purpose to free them."—(*Emory's History of the Discipline*, pp. 43, 44.)

Let not the reader fail to remember that this extirpatory law was enacted *at the very founding of the Methodist Episcopal Church*, and incorporated into *the first Methodist Discipline ever published in America.* Mark, also, its provisions—the notice in the circuits, the book of recorded manumissions, the absolute prohibition of slaveholders from entering the Church, the course taken with infants, &c. Even the "N. B." paragraph only arrested the operation of the rule where legal emancipations were impossible, the State laws forbidding it.

Such, in the beginning, was the testimony of the Methodist Episcopal Church against slavery. Practical abolitionism had a large place in its very foundations. For more than forty years Methodism had battled with the monster, first in England, and then in the New World. Chief ministers had been threatened and indicted, and hunted with deadly weapons, but still they maintained their anti-slavery principles, and were resolved to "extirpate the abomination from among them." So far as slavery is concerned, these first forty-five years of her history, from 1739 to 1784, were her purest and brightest days. The sun of her moral glory culminated at the "Christmas Conference," 1784. She had triumphed in England, and 800,000 emancipated bondmen were the living and joyful witnesses of her power. In America, also, scores of once enslaved, but now free sons and daughters of Africa, were rejoicing in the liberty wherewith Methodism had made them free.

Taking in the period from 1739 to 1830, it may be said of her, that her FOUNDER was an abolitionist; her WATSON, and CLARKE, and BRADBURN, were abolitionists; her thousands of children in England were abolitionists; her first two bishops in America, COKE and ASBURY, were abolitionists; her GARRETTSON was an abolitionist; her MCKENDREE was an abolitionist; the members of the first Conferences held in this country were generally abolitionists; and the very founders of our Church, in Baltimore, in 1784, were a body of most earnest abolitionist preachers. At its very erection, the Methodist Episcopal Church was cemented from foundation to top-stone, with the well-tempered mortar of what is now sneeringly called "modern abolitionism." No man living can deny it. The original platform of Methodism was an abolition platform, and pro-slavery is the innovation and the apostasy, the hideous excrescence. May the Lord help us to ask for the old paths, the good way, and walk therein.

CHAPTER II

DOWNWARD PROGRESS OF THE CHURCH, IN REGARD TO SLAVERY, FROM 1784 AND ONWARD.

WE have seen, in the preceding chapter, the glorious position taken by the Methodist Episcopal Church at her very commencement. Would to Heaven we could now proceed to show how gloriously she maintained it! But this pleasure is denied us. From this golden epoch in our history, our testimony and efforts grew more and more feeble, till they became like the voice and the efforts of an infant. True, this downward progress was not rapid at the first; but, nevertheless, perceptible and accelerated. As the light of the sun, when near the meridian, is not perceptibly diminished by his westward progress, still he is on the way to the horizon, and the dial indicates his downward march.

We have seen, on pages 12, 13, how zealously and fearlessly Dr. Coke labored for the extirpation of slavery, and the carrying out of the Rule of 1784. He not only preached on the subject, and thus procured in one instance the liberation of several slaves; but also endeavored to secure a modification of the laws of North Carolina, so that the Rule of the Conference might be brought to bear upon the slaveholding Methodists of that province also. Then, as now, reproving slavery in its midst, drew a storm of persecution after it, and the following will show how resolutely the demands of slavery were at first resisted.

ONSET OF THE SLAVE-POWER.

"At a Conference held in this State [Virginia, April, 1785], many of the principal friends of Methodism assembled from various quarters, to urge the necessity of suspending the operation of the Rule against slavery, which had created so much uneasiness; and which, if persisted in, they were apprehensive would ultimately render Methodism unproductive of any public advantage. But although these pleas were specious, Dr. Coke and his friends were not to be proselyted by them. It was, therefore, brought to this issue, that unless the Rules against slavery were permitted to operate, since it was founded upon principles of immutable justice, and supported by reason, by the moral feelings of the heart, and by the powerful voice of Revelation, preaching should be withdrawn altogether from those circuits and places in which it was too obnoxious to be suffered.

"Astonished at these determinations, the opposers of the Rule began seriously to weigh the opposite members of the alternative, to one of which they were compelled to submit. And finding, how desirable soever it might be to preserve the Gospel in peace, that it would be attended with more serious inconvenience to lose it altogether, though connected with its Rule against slavery, they withdrew their opposition. A letter was accordingly addressed to the Conference, expressive of their resolution, and praying for the reappointment of the preachers," &c.—(*Life of Coke*, pp. 135, 136.)

Let the reader mark two things in the above—the noble stand of Dr. Coke, *a whole Gospel or none;* and the *yielding of the slave interest* when they found him determined. So it should have been, and we believe *might* have been, had the same determination been steadfastly persisted in. But, alas! for poor human nature!

FIRST STEP DOWNWARD.

On the second of June following—only two months after this noble stand was taken—another Conference met in Baltimore; the slave-power doubtless rallied again; and the following note was inserted in the Discipline:

"It is recommended to all our brethren to suspend the execution of the minute on slavery, *till the deliberations of a future Conference;* and that an equal space of time be allowed all our members for consideration, when the minute shall be put in force.

"N. B. We do hold in the deepest abhorrence the practice of slavery, and shall not cease to seek its destruction, by all wise and prudent means." —(*Hist. of Dis.* pp. 274, 275.)

Here is not only an expression of their deep abhorrence of slavery, but the expression of a determination to put the minute in force at some future day. Still it was a *yielding* on the part of the Conference, and a victory for slavery. The Rules were never again restored, and were soon left out of the Discipline.

From 1785 to 1796 no mention, it would seem, was made of the subject, except that the paragraph relating to slavery remained in the General Rules, as inserted in 1784.

SECOND STEP DOWNWARD.

In 1792 the language of the General Rule against slavery, adopted in 1784, was materially softened. Instead of forbidding "the buying or selling the bodies and souls of men," &c., it was made to read, "the buying or selling of men," &c.; not "the bodies and souls," &c.; thus taking off the coloring which the original Rule cast upon the slave traffic.

SCREW TURNED THE OTHER WAY.

In 1796 the anti-slavery spirit developed itself more strongly again, and the following Rules were adopted, and inserted in the Discipline:

"*Quest.* What regulations shall be made for the extirpation of the crying evil of African slavery?

"*Ans.* 1. We declare that we are more than ever convinced of the great evil of African slavery, which still exists in these United States, and do most earnestly recommend to the Yearly Conferences, Quarterly Meetings, and to those who have the oversight of Districts and Circuits, to be exceedingly cautious what persons they admit to official stations in our Church; and in the case of future admission to official stations, to require such security of those who hold slaves, for the emancipation of them, immediately, or gradually, as the laws of the States respectively, and the circumstances of the case will admit; and we do fully authorize all the Yearly Conferences to make whatever regulations they judge proper, in the present case, respecting the admission of persons to official stations in our Church.

"2. No slaveholder shall be received into Society till the preacher who has the oversight of the Circuit, has spoken to him freely and faithfully upon the subject of slavery.

"3 Every member of the Society who sells a slave, shall immediately, after full proof, be excluded from the Society; and if any member of our Society purchase a slave, the ensuing Quarterly Meeting shall determine on the number of years in which the slave so purchased would work out the price of his purchase. And the person so purchasing, shall immediately after such determination, execute a legal instrument for the manumission such slave at the expiration of the term determined by the Quarterly Meeting. And in default of his executing such instrument of manumission, or on his refusal to submit his case to the judgment of the Quarterly Meeting, such member shall be excluded from the Society. Provided also, that in the case of a female slave, it shall be inserted in the aforesaid instrument of manumission, that all her children who shall be born during the years of her servitude, shall be free at the following times, namely:—every female child at the age of *twenty-one*, and every male child at the age of *twenty-five*. Nevertheless, if the member of our Society, executing the said instrument of manumission, judge it proper, he may fix the times of manumission of the female slaves before mentioned, at an earlier age than that which is prescribed above.

"4. The preachers and other members of our Society, are requested to consider the subject of negro slavery with deep attention; and that they impart to the General Conference, through the medium of the Yearly Conferences, or otherwise, any important thoughts upon the subject, that the Conference may have full light in order to take further steps towards the eradicating this enormous evil from that part of the Church of God to which they are connected."—(*Hist. of Dis.* p. 275.)

Mark the language of this new law. They were "*more* than ever convinced of the *crying evil* of African slavery"—*not* the foreign traffic, but that which "still existed in these United States."

This New Rule was vigorously enforced for a time, and under its operation no doubt hundreds of slaves were manumitted. We have before us an old smoky MS. Journal of the Quarterly Meeting Conference of Dorchester Circuit, Md., which illustrates its practical operation, as no published records have ever done.

On the inside of the front cover are the words "R. Benson, Jan. 13, '96;" and the first three leaves, which, no doubt, contained the record from 1796 to 1804, and some offensive abolition matter, have been cut out. The first record still remaining is of a Quarterly Meeting held March 3d, 1804, and contains the following:

FRUITS OF THE NEW RULE.

"Levin Lecompt having purchased a negro girl named Cloe, for which he gave the sum of two hundred dollars, and having submitted the matter to Conference, they thereupon determined that said Levin Lecompt shall make and record a regular manumission for said girl previous to the next Quarterly Meeting, and that he shall be authorized to hold the said girl for the term of twelve years from the first day of January last past. Died."

The following are also copied from the record of the proceedings of Quarterly Conferences, under the several dates respectively:

April 6, 1805.—"The case of Joseph Meekins, who has purchased a negro woman and child, was considered. *Resolved*, That the said negro woman shall serve eight years, and the said boy named Ben shall serve until he is twenty-six years old. Expelled for non-compliance."

"The case of Samuel Cook, who had purchased a negro woman named Henney, was considered. *Resolved*, That the said woman shall serve fourteen years from the time of her purchase."

"The case of Ezekiel Vickars, who had purchased a negro man named Sawney, was considered. *Resolved*, That the said negro man shall serve four years from the time of his purchase."

"*Resolved*, That certificates be produced at the next Quarterly Meeting Conference, by the several persons aforesaid, of their compliance with the aforesaid resolves."

July 12, 1805.—"*Resolved*, That in future all certificates of manumission shall be returned to the Conference within six months."

"The case of George Travers, who had bought a negro man named Roger, aged about 25 years, for whom he gave $318, was considered; and *Resolved*, That he manumit said negro to be free at the expiration of nine years from the time of the purchase."

December 6, 1805.—"In the case of Levin Saunders, who purchased a negro man named Jacob, at £90—*Resolved*, That Jacob may be held to serve until the first day of January, 1814; and a child, name or sex not mentioned, laid over to next Quarterly Meeting Conference, when said Saunders must also bring forward the case of a manumitted woman which he has also purchased."

March 14, 1806.—"*Resolved*, That the Conference will not review the case of manumitted before decided on. Joseph Summer's case was considered, who had purchased two negroes, viz., Joseph Viney, aged 19 years, and James Viney, aged 10 years, the cost of which two negroes was £123 15*s.*

"*Resolved*, That they both be held to serve till they each arrive to 25 years of age."

"The case of Daniel Martin was considered, who had purchased a negro named Ben, 16 years old, for £75. *Resolved*, That Ben may be held to serve until he be 25 years old."

"The case of Job Wheatley was considered, who had purchased a negro girl named Rose, 14 years old, for £30. *Resolved*, That Rose may be held to serve till she is 21 years old."

"The case of Walter Rawleigh was considered, who had purchased a negro named Moses, 23 years old, for £100. *Resolved*, That the said Moses may be held to serve ten years from the time he was purchased."

"The case of Henry Traverse was considered, who had purchased a negro named David, 23 years old, for £90. *Resolved*, That the said David may be held to serve nine years from the time of purchase."

"The case of Henry Arnett was considered, who had purchased a negro 50 years old, named James Hicks, for $10. *Resolved*, That James may be held to serve two years from the time of purchase."

"The case of Levin Saunders, brought forward from last Conference, was considered. *Resolved*, That the woman named Minty, who, by former manumission, is to serve six years and nine months, may be held to serve her full time out; and the child named Ritty, two years old, shall serve until 21 years old."

'The case of Ezekiel Vickars was considered, who had purchased a negro named James Blake, 21 years old, for £88. *Resolved*, That James may be held to serve eight years from January last."

"*Resolved*, That the Secretary send a statement to each person concerned in the negro business."

Thus, we have *eight cases* at this one Conference!

June 20, 1806.—"Roger Robertson's case was considered, who had sold a negro for life, alleging ignorance of the rules of the Society. *Resolved*, That he be disowned as a member."

"Ez. Vickars, Walter Rawleigh, Job Whitely, Sam. Cook, and James Summers gave satisfactory assurances to the Conference, that they had complied with the resolves of last Conference respecting the manumission of their slaves."

September 5, 1806.—"Nathaniel Lecompt submitted his case to the Conference. *Resolved*, That he manumit his negro girl Lotty, to be free January 1, 1817, and return a certificate, &c."

November 14, 1806.—"The case of Peggy Turnbul was considered, who had purchased a female slave, named Sal, aged eight years, for which she gave $85. *Resolved*, That the said girl serve until she be 21 years of age.'

"The case of Henry Traverse was considered, who had purchased a female slave, named Milly, aged 23 years, for which he gave $220. *Resolved*, That the said girl may be held to serve sixteen years."

February 27, 1807.—"Nathan Steven's case was heard, who had bought a negro girl, four years old next June, named Sarah, price $50. *Determined*, That Sarah may be held to serve until she be 21 years old."

"The Traverse case was heard, who had purchased a negro woman, named Alse, aged 30 years, price $100. *Determined*, That she may be held to serve seven years, from the time of purchase."

"Michael Fitchett's case was heard, who had purchased a negro boy, named Levin, aged 10 years, price £55. *Determined*, That he may be held to serve until he is 25 years old."

"Thomas Simmons' case was heard, who had purchased two negroes, viz.: Sarah, aged 14 years, price £57 10; and Elisha, aged 12 years, price £60. *Determined*, That Sarah may be held to serve until she is 25 years old, and Elisha, until 25 years old."

"Francis Mibb's case was heard, who had purchased a negro boy, named John, aged 13 years, price $40. *Determined*, That he may be held to serve until 25 years old."

October 1, 1808.—"Roger Cooper's case, who had purchased a negro man, aged 37 years, for whom he gave $250, being submitted. *Resolved*, That the said negro may be held to serve for seven years from next Christmas."

March 31, 1810.—"Michael Fitchett, who had purchased a negro man, for which he gave $300, submits his case to the Conference. *Resolved*, That he may hold said negro for ten years from the time of purchase."

"Charles R. Bryan, who had purchased a negro girl, for which he gave $100, submits his case to the Conference. *Resolved*, That he may hold said girl until she is 25 years old."

July 21, 1810.*—"Joseph Dodson, having bought a negro man, requests

* Under this date we have a copy of the "Report of the Committee on the slave

the advice of the Conference, when he shall set him free. *Resolved*, That they recommend him to be set free at the expiration of five years from the first of January next."

August 6, 1814.—"On examination, it was found the said Daniel held slaves, and not willing to give assurance of their emancipation, the Conference refused to grant him license."

February 23, 1816.—"Paul Connoway's case, who had purchased a negro woman and child, was submitted to Thomas Foster and Geo. Ward, chosen by the said Conway, John Seward, and Samuel Cook, chosen by the preacher, who conjointly chose Wm. Weller, who, all having heard and considered all circumstances, determined that Paul Connoway execute a manumission of the aforesaid negroes; the woman to be free at the end of five years from the first day of January last, and the boy to be free when he shall have completed his twenty-eighth year."

This is the last entry in the book respecting slavery, though the record extends to May 2, 1829. For the last thirteen years, it preserves the most profound silence upon the subject, showing that after a long struggle, from the first fatal compromise in 1784 to 1810, slavery at last triumphed, and the voice of the "Quarterly Meeting Conference of Dorchester Circuit, Md.," against it, was hushed forever. (By the way, this "Dorchester Circuit," is still within the bounds of the Philadelphia Conference, and is the very region from which Rev. Mr. Lame, a member of that Conference, was banished but a few months since, for writing against slavery, of which, more hereafter.)

"PROPERTY" SACRIFICED FOR METHODISM.

The preceding record shows very clearly that at the beginning, Methodist preachers and Conferences were practical abolitionists. Speaking of this period, Rev. Mr. DeVinne says:

"Our northern apologists and historians have mistaken the knowledge of this period of our history. How often have I heard aged members of our Church at the South, lament the awful *dereliction* of principle in this case, since the time of their first union with the Church. To use their own language, they had made themselves poor by the unconditional emancipation of their slaves, to obtain a standing in the Methodist Episcopal Church, but that they had lived to see that very Church vitiated and overrun with slavery and oppression of their brethren."

But to go back a little in our narrative. In 1796, Bishops Coke and Asbury published their notes on the Discipline, in which we find the following on the General Rule on slavery:

---

business," made at the Easton Conference, &c., and inserted on a subsequent page of this work; and under date of May 14, 1814, a copy of an "Extract from the Journal of the Philadelphia Conference," also given hereafter.

"The buying and selling the souls and bodies of men (for what is the body without the soul but a dead mass?) is a complicated crime. It was, indeed, *in some measure*, overlooked in the Jews, by reason of the wonderful hardness of their hearts, as was the keeping of concubines and divorcing of wives at pleasure; but is totally opposite to the whole spirit of the Gospel. It has an immediate tendency to fill the mind with pride and tyranny, and is frequently productive of almost every act of lust and cruelty which can disgrace the human species. Even the moral philosopher will candidly confess, that if there be a God, every perfection he possesses must be opposed to a practice so contrary to every moral idea which can influence the human mind."—(*Hist. of Dis.* p. 326.)

ANOTHER STEP TAKEN.

In 1800, the following new paragraphs were inserted among the rules adopted in 1796, and given on page 24, viz.:

"When any travelling preacher becomes an owner of a slave, or slaves, *by any means*, he shall forfeit his ministerial character in our Church, unless he executes, if it be practicable, a legal emancipation of such slaves, conformably to the laws of the State in which he lives."

This year, also, we have the following:

"Brother Lathomus moved, that every member of the Methodist Episcopal Church, holding slaves, shall, within the term of one year from the date hereof, give an instrument of emancipation for all his slaves; and the Quarterly Meeting Conference shall determine on the time the slave shall serve, if the laws of the State do not expressly prohibit their emancipation. Negatived."—(*Journals of General Conference*, vol. i. p. 14.)

"The Annual Conferences are directed to draw up addresses for the gradual emancipation of the slaves, to the legislatures of those States in which no general laws have been passed for that purpose. These addresses shall urge, in the most respectful, but pointed manner, the necessity of a law for the gradual emancipation of the slaves; proper committees shall be appointed by the Annual Conferences, out of the most respectable of our friends, for the conducting of the business; and the presiding elders, deacons, and travelling preachers, shall procure as many proper signatures as possible to the addresses, and give all the assistance in their power, in every respect, to aid the committees, and to further this blessed undertaking. *Let this be continued from year to year till the desired end be accomplished.*"—(*Hist. of Dis.* p. 276.)

THIRD STEP DOWNWARD.

In 1804, the section on slavery, adopted in 1896 (see page 24), was materially toned down. For "the crying evil of American" slavery, we have "the evil," &c., as if it was not a "crying" evil. For "more than ever convinced," they substituted "as much as ever convinced;" and instead of "the African slavery which still exists in these United States," we have merely the word "slavery." Several other amendments of the Rule were made at this Conference, among which was the "exemption of the societies in North and South Carolina, Georgia, and Tennessee," from the operation of the Rule, the striking out of the paragraph, added in 1800, respecting petitions, &c. (see above), and the insertion of the following in its place:

"Let our preachers, from time to time, as occasion serves, admonish and exhort all slaves to render due respect and obedience to the commands and interests of their respective masters."—(*See Journals*, pp. 60, 62, 83.)

They had now ceased to testify to the masters against the "execrable villany" of holding slaves, and gone to preaching to the slaves to submit to their oppressors!

FOURTH STEP DOWNWARD.

In 1808, all that related to slaveholding among private members (Sec. 2 and 3 of 1796) was stricken out, and the following put in its place:

"The General Conference authorizes each Annual Conference to form their own regulations, relative to buying and selling slaves."

What a stride downward was here! It was not the *holding* of slaves that each Conference was to regulate, but the "buying and selling." And to clear the track, they also struck out paragraph 5, of the Rules of 1804, so that there was nothing left in the Discipline against buying and selling slaves, except the General Rule on the subject.—(*Hist.* p. 578.)

This year the General Rule against slavery was again tampered with, not by the Conference, but by some unknown hand. Instead of reading, as heretofore, "The buying *or* selling," &c., it was made to read, "The buying *and* selling," &c.; putting "and" in the place of "or" all the way through; so that a person must buy and sell two men, two women, and two children, in order to violate the Rule!

SLAVERY TRIUMPHANT.

From this time the tide of slavery swept onward with resistless fury. Methodism had made her peace with it, except so far as to keep slaveholders out of the ministry, and out of official stations, such as Leaderships, &c.; and thus it spread over the Southern States, gathering slaveholders by thousands into the Methodist Episcopal Church. Her ministers having ceased to preach against slavery as in former years, were no more persecuted on that account; "AMERICAN SLAVERY—the vilest that ever saw the sun"*—was fairly baptized and introduced into the Church of Wesley and Coke, and Asbury and Garrettson! Could angels have wept, they would have bedewed the very graves of these holy men with their tears from heaven, in view of this disgraceful compromise with sin! What a sad and terrible apostasy from the exalted position of former years!

This year, also, an attempt was made by Stephen G. Roszel to modify the Rule still further; and T. L. Budd moved to strike the whole section out of the Discipline. (*Journal*, vol. i. p. 93.) But neither of these attempts succeeded.

SLIGHT RESISTANCE AGAIN.

Under date of July 21, 1810, we find the following in the old record of the Quarterly Meeting Conference of Dorchester Circuit, Maryland, described on page 25:

"*Resolved*, That the 'Report of the Committee on the Slave Business,' made at the Eastern Conference (being the Annual Conference for this and the other districts in conferential connection with this) last spring, be inserted on the records of this Conference, viz.:

"1st. That every preacher and every Quarterly Meeting Conference be advised, and they are hereby advised, to use all their lawful and prudential influence to promote the freedom of slaves.

"2d. That they be further advised and requested not to give license to any persons, who come forward in future to preach or exhort, who hold slaves, excepting they give assurances that their slaves shall be emancipated if the laws will admit of it.

"3d. That the preachers be requested in all future apointments of class-leaders, not to appoint any who are unfriendly to the freedom of slaves.

"4th. That every member of our Church who sells a slave into perpetual slavery, shall be called to a trial, as in cases of immorality."

Under date of May 14, 1814, we have the following interesting extract from the Journals of the Philadelphia Conference. It is taken from the same old record already described. We commend it to the consideration of those members of that body, who accuse some of their anti-slavery brethren of being innovators, &c.

"*Extract from the Journal of the Philadelphia Conference.* If any member of our Church purchase a slave or slaves, the preacher having the charge of the circuit or station where such member may belong, shall nominate two white male members of our Society, and call upon such purchaser to nominate two others, which four persons shall nominate a fifth, and those five persons shall form a committee, who shall determine on the time such slave or slaves shall serve such purchaser, who shall execute and

---

* John Wesley.

have recorded a deed of manumission accordingly, in which manumission, if the slaves be females, provision shall be made for the freedom of any child or children of such slave or slaves, which may be born after the purchase, to be free either immediately after birth, or at furthest the female children within twenty-one, and the male children within twenty-five years after their birth. But if such purchaser be dissatisfied with the decision of the committee, he may appeal to the next Quarterly Meeting Conference of that circuit or station, and the decision of such Conference in the case shall be final. And if such purchaser refuse either to submit to this course, or to comply with the decision of the committee, or with the decision of the Quarterly Meeting Conference in case of appeal, he shall be expelled the Society. Nevertheless, this Rule shall not be executed in any place, further than the laws of the State, in which such place may be, will admit of.

"Signed in behalf of the Conference.

"*April* 16, 1814."

FIFTH STEP DOWNWARD.

In 1820, J. Axley, seconded by L. McCombs, offered the following resolution in the General Conference:

"*Resolved*, &c., That no person shall hereafter be licensed as a local preacher or exhorter, nor shall the Annual Conferences receive any one as a travelling preacher on trial, or into the travelling connection, who holds slaves."

Though pending before the Conference on adjournment, May 22, yet when they met the next day, it was not called up; other business was crowded in by "Br. Roszel," and thus it was given the go-by.—(*Journal*, vol. i. p. 228.)

SIXTH STEP DOWNWARD.

A few years afterwards, even this Br. Roszel seems to have seen the fruit of his mistaken policy. Hence, on the 17th of May, 1828, he offered the following, seconded by P. W. Cartwright:

"*Resolved*, by the Delegates of the Annual Conference in General Conference assembled, That in all cases when there is credible testimony against any members, showing that they treat their slave or slaves with inhumanity, either in not supplying them with comfortable and sufficient food or raiment, or in separating husbands and wives or parents and children, by buying or selling them in an inhuman traffic of our fellow-creatures, the person or persons so offending shall be dealt with in the same manner as in the cases of immorality; and that this regulation be inserted in our form of Discipline."

Observe now, that this resolution did not bear upon *slaveholding* as such, either by ministers or private members; but upon what are called, in modern parlance, "the *evils* of slavery." And yet it was summarily "laid on the table!" The Conference refused even to *consider* a proposition to forbid the inhuman treatment of the poor bondmen and bondwomen held by the membership of the Church!—(See *Journal*, vol. i. p. 337.)

STONING THE PROPHETS.

At the General Conference held in Cincinnati, in 1836, the following preamble and resolutions were adopted, on motion of S. G. Roszel:

"Whereas great excitement has pervaded this country on the subject of modern abolitionism, which is reported to have been increased in this city, recently, by the unjustifiable conduct of two members of the General Conference, in lecturing upon, and in favor of that agitating topic;—and whereas, such a course on the part of any of its members is calculated to bring upon this body the suspicion and distrust of the community, and misrepresent its sentiments in regard to the point at issue;—and whereas, in this aspect of the case, a due regard for its own character, as well as a just concern for the interests of the Church confided to its care, demand a full, decided, and unequivocal expression of the views of the General Conference in the premises,—Therefore,

"1. *Resolved*, by the delegates of the Annual Conferences in General Conference assembled, That they disapprove, in the most unqualified sense, the conduct of the two members of the General Conference, who are reported to have lectured in this city recently, upon and in favor of modern abolitionism.

"2. *Resolved*, by the delegates of the Annual Conferences in General Conference assembled, That they are decidedly opposed to modern abolitionism, and wholly disclaim any right, wish or intention, to interfere in the civil and political relation between master and slave, as it exists in the slaveholding States of this Union."—(*Journal*, vol. i. p. 447.)

The "two members" thus censured were Geo. Storrs and Wm. Norris of New England, who had attended a regular weekly meeting of the Cincinnati Anti-Slavery Society, a few evenings before, and taken part in its proceedings.

ALL STEADY AND QUIET AGAIN.

At the same Conference a committee on slavery reported, that "it would be highly improper for the General Conference to take any action that would alter or change our Rules on the subject of slavery;" and adopted the following resolution:

"*Resolved*, That it is inexpedient to make any change in our book of Discipline respecting slavery, and that we deem it improper further to agitate the subject in the General Conference at present."—(*Journal*, vol. i. p. 475.)

OFFICIALLY ADVISED NOT TO AGITATE.

This Conference also issued a Pastoral Address, signed by the bishops, exhorting the Church "to abstain from all abolition movements and associations; to refrain from patronizing any of their publications;" and to "wholly refrain from the agitating subject."

A DEEPER PLUNGE DOWNWARD.

Not long previous to the General Conference of 1840, Rev. S. Comfort, then of Missouri Conference, but now of Oneida, was charged with maladministration, for allowing a colored person to testify in a Church trial, and appealed to the General Conference. When his appeal came up, Ignatius A. Few offered the following resolution, which was seconded by Dr. George Peck, and adopted by the Conference, 74 to 46:

"*Resolved*, That it is inexpedient and unjustifiable, for any preacher among us, to permit colored persons to give testimony against white persons, in any State where they are denied that privilege in trials at law."—(*Journal*, vol. ii. p. 60.)

STILL DOWNWARD—SLAVEHOLDING ALLOWED IN THE MINISTRY.

At this General Conference, a memorial was presented from fifteen official members of Westmoreland Circuit, Baltimore Conference, complaining that ordination had been withheld from some of their local preachers, merely because they were slaveholders. This memorial was referred to a committee of nine, and a report presented and adopted, which concludes with the following resolution:

"*Resolved*, By the delegates of the several Annual Conferences in General Conference Assembled, that, under the provisional exception of the general rule of the Church on the subject of slavery, the simple holding of slaves, or mere ownership of slave property, in States or territories where the laws do not admit of emancipation and permit the liberated slave to enjoy freedom, constitutes no legal barrier to the election or ordination of ministers to the various grades of office known in the ministry of the Methodist Episcopal Church; and cannot, therefore, be considered as operating any forfeiture of right in view of such election and ordination."—(*Journal*, vol. ii. pp. 167–171.)

This resolution greatly encouraged and emboldened the slave-power in the Church, and its evil effects were very soon apparent.

A STILL LOWER DEPTH—A SLAVEHOLDING BISHOP.

The General Conference of 1840 had so far endorsed the doctrine that slaveholding should be no bar to the ministry, that the way seemed quite clear, so far as the views of that body were concerned, for the ministry generally to go into "the slave business." It is not strange, therefore, that at their next session, 1844, Rev. James O. Andrew, one of the bishops of the Methodist Episcopal Church, was found to be a slaveholder. This brought the General Conference to a dead stand. They must either do *something* with Bishop Andrew, or openly tolerate slaveholding in the highest dignitaries of the Church. Some action was rendered the more imperative, from the fact that the position taken by the General Conference of 1840, in regard to colored testimony and slaveholding local preachers, had precipitated a secession at the North, and the organization of the Wesleyan Methodist Church only a year before. The Conference was therefore constrained, either to notice the connection of Bishop Andrew with slavery, or encourage still further secession.

The bishops united in an Address to the Conference, "recommending the postponement of further action in the case of Bishop Andrew until the ensuing General Conference."—(*Journal for* 1844, p. 75.) But the Conference were not willing to let the matter rest thus, and finally adopted the following, by a vote of 110 to 68:

> "*Whereas*, The Discipline of our Church forbids the doing any thing calculated to destroy our itinerant general superintendency; and whereas Bishop Andrew has become connected with slavery by marriage and otherwise, and this act having drawn after it circumstances which, in the estimation of the General Conference, will greatly embarrass the exercise of his office as an itinerant general superintendent, if not in some places entirely prevent it; therefore,
>
> "*Resolved*, That it is the sense of this General Conference, that he desist from the exercise of his office, so long as this impediment remains."—(*Journal for* 1844, pp. 65, 66.)

No complaint is here made on moral grounds against episcopal slaveholding. It is solely on the ground that a slaveholding bishop would not be well received in New England and other Northern States. Besides, the bishop was left a bishop still—aye, and a slaveholding bishop, with his name in the Discipline and Hymn-book, and drawing his salary the same as other bishops. It is worthy of note, also, that all the delegates from the Missouri Conference, said to be so intensely anti-slavery just now, voted *against* the above resolution, thus actually *approving* of slavery in the episcopacy.

RESULT OF THE PRECEDING ACTION.

The southern delegates, finding that a slight check was about to be put upon slavery, so far as the episcopacy was concerned, first protested, then got a plan of separation adopted, and finally went home and seceded, taking with them most of the membership in the slaveholding States. In due time they sued the Book Agents, and pro-slavery judges gave them a large share of the Church property; and they now constitute the "Methodist Episcopal Church South," and are breeding, buying, selling, owning, and whipping negroes to their hearts' content, having stripped every thing out of the Discipline that would even forbid their bishops from going into the African slave-trade.

Thus, from 1784 to 1844, the standard of anti-slavery in the Methodist Episcopal Church had been going down, *down*, DOWN, till that which was once disallowed in the most humble private member, was now openly tolerated in a Methodist bishop! To be sure, the Conference had confirmed the action of the Baltimore Conference in suspending F. A. Harding, one of their preachers, for holding slaves, but they left Bishop Andrew a bishop still, with his name enrolled with others as such, and receiving a salary like the rest, for episcopal services.

DR. DURBIN A WITNESS.

Speaking upon the case of Bishop Andrew, Dr. Durbin said:

"We have had some strange statements here in regard to the legislation of the Church on the subject of slavery. Brethren have tried to make the impression, to use one of their own figures, that the North has been putting the screws on the South, and continually pressing them harder, until at last the compression can be endured no longer. Sir, the facts in the case are just the reverse of all this. The history of the Church shows this point indisputably, that the highest ground that has ever been held upon the subject was taken at the very organization of the Church, and that concessions have been made by the Church continually, from that time to this, in view of the *necessities* of the South; that while the anti-slavery principle has never been abandoned, our rules have been made less and less stringent, and our language less and less severe."

On the 7th of April, 1847, the Philadelphia Conference, then in session at Wilmington, Delaware, addressed a special Pastoral Address to the slaveholders of Northampton and Accomac counties, Virginia, disclaiming all anti-slavery tendencies; professing to be as pro-slavery as the Southern Church; pointing to their antecedents in proof of their conservatism; and entreating them to remain quietly with the Northern portion of the Church. This address is entitled "Pastoral Address of the Philadelphia Annual Conference of the Methodist Episcopal Church, to the Societies under its care within the bounds of the Northampton and Accomac Circuits, dated April 7, 1847."

In this remarkable Address we find the following very explicit passages:

"We learn that the simple cause of the unhappy excitement among you is, that some suspect us, or affect to suspect us, of being abolitionists. Yet no particular act of the Conference, or any particular member thereof, is adduced as the ground of the erroneous and injurious suspicion. We would ask you, brethren, whether the conduct of our ministry among you for sixty years past ought not to be sufficient to protect us from this charge—whether the question we have been accustomed, for a few years past, to put to candidates for admission among us, namely, *Are you an abolitionist?* and without each one answered in the negative he was not received, ought not to protect us from the charge—whether the action of the last Conference on this particular matter ought not to satisfy any fair and candid mind that we are not, and do not desire to be abolitionists? The views and purposes of the last Conference to which we refer, were expressed in the words below, which we must believe have not been generally read in your community, or the apprehensions which have been so earnestly expressed would never have been entertained. The words of the Conference are:

"'The committee, to whom was referred a certain preamble and resolution on the subject of slavery and abolition, recommend the following report:

"'That we, the members of the Philadelphia Annual Conference, are as much as ever convinced of the great evil of slavery; but at the same time we know our calling too well to interfere with matters not properly belonging to the Christian ministry. We stand, in relation to slavery and abolition, where we have always stood, and where we expect to stand, 'walking by the same rule and minding the same things;' and ask that our action in the past may be taken as an index to our action in the future; therefore,

"'1. *Resolved*, That we will abide by the Discipline of the Methodist Episcopal Church as it is; and will resist every attempt to alter it in reference to slavery, so as to change the terms of membership.

"'2. *Resolved*, That we sincerely deprecate all agitation of the exciting subjects which have unhappily divided the Church; and, impressed with the vital importance, especially for these times, of the apostolic injunction, 'Be at peace among yourselves,' we will, as far as lies in our power, 'follow peace with all men, and holiness, without which no man shall see the Lord.'

"'Upon presenting this paper to you, in which we say, 'We stand, in relation to slavery and abolition, where we have always stood,' it is proper that we should remind you of the fact, that the provisions in the Discipline of the Methodist Episcopal Church, and of the Methodist Episcopal Church South, with respect to slavery, are precisely the same, even to the very words. We cannot, therefore, see how we can be regarded as abolitionists, without the ministers of the Methodist Episcopal Church South being considered in the same light,' &c.

"Wishing you all heavenly benediction, we are, dear brethren, yours in Christ.

J. P. Durbin,
J. Kennady,
Ignatius T. Cooper,
Wm. H. Guilder,
Joseph Castle,
Committee."*

"Wilmington, Del., *April* 7, 1847."

* History of the Great Secession, by Dr. Elliott, p. 1083, Document 72.

How distinctly the Philadelphia Conference shook out their pro-slavery colors in this Address! Its sole object, most obviously, was to conciliate the slaveholders of Northampton and Accomac counties, Virginia, by convincing them that they, the Conference, were just as pro-slavery as the Church South, and would never disturb them in their abominable iniquities. And the sequel has proved that the Conference have kept their pledge, as subsequent pages will sorrowfully bear witness.

ANTI-SLAVERY SLAVEHOLDING.

The Pastoral Address of the General Conference of 1856 not only declared that "little or no mercenary slaveholding exists in the Church," but that "none of the members of this [that] General Conference entertained pro-slavery sentiments."* Indeed, the border delegates repeatedly declared themselves to be "anti-slavery;" and in that same address the Methodist Episcopal Church, with thousands of slaves held by her membership, and hundreds of leaders, and stewards, and exhorters, and local preachers, and even some travelling preachers, holding slaves (as we shall soon show), solemnly wiped her mouth and said: "*Our position, from the beginning, has been that of an anti-slavery Church; and in both slave and free States* THIS IS OUR PRESENT ATTITUDE."† It was useless, as things were drifting when that address was reported and adopted (but Heaven knows without our act)—it was useless to object, or even raise a question; but we thought of the terrible words of Jehovah to ancient Israel—"Though thou wash thee with nitre, and take thee much soap [the soap of frothy *declaration* and profession of innocence], yet thine iniquity is marked before me, saith the Lord God."‡

BALTIMORE "ANTI-SLAVERY."

Well, the Conference adjourned, and the "anti-slavery" delegation from "Old Baltimore" went home, and the first time they come together as a Conference, March 17, 1857, they express their "anti-slavery" in the following resolutions:

"*Resolved*, By the Baltimore Conference, in Conference assembled, that we highly deprecate the agitation of the slavery question, which has already resulted to the great detriment of the political and religious interests of the country.

"*Resolved*, That, as heretofore, we will oppose with zeal any aggression which shall be attempted by the abolition agitations of the country."

* Printed Journal, p. 297. † Ibid. ‡ Jeremiah, ii. 22.

Of nearly four hundred "anti-slavery" preachers in the Conference, only fourteen voted against these resolutions. Such is the "anti-slavery" of the Border Conferences.

Speaking of the passage of these resolutions, Rev. J. D. Long has the following pertinent and eloquent remarks:

"The first resolution deprecates the agitation of slavery. Observe carefully. The Conference does not deprecate *slavery*, but it deprecates *resistance* to the *aggressions* of slavery. The Conference does not deprecate the fact that four millions of our brethren are in hopeless and worse than Egyptian bondage; that they are increasing at the fearful rate of one hundred thousand a year; that the day on which they passed the resolution two hundred and fifty human-beings came into the world with the slaveholder's *brand of infamy* upon them. The Conference did not deprecate the introduction of slavery into Kansas, the late inhuman and anti-Christian decision of the majority of the Supreme Court in the case of Dred Scott, the existence of the slave-pens in the very city in which they were assembled. Perhaps at the very time they were debating the above resolutions, several of their brethren in Christ were being handcuffed and marched down to some ship bound for Charleston or New Orleans; husbands were parted from wives to whom they were united by some of the very preachers who were pledging themselves zealously to oppose all denunciation of the infamous traffic in human flesh; children were separated from their mothers, though offered to the Lord in holy consecration, and baptized, perhaps, by these very ministers, in the name of the Holy Trinity. Yes! that very hour, perhaps, violated females of the Methodist, Presbyterian, Baptist, and Episcopal Churches were crying to God for mercy and support, while their *shepherds* were *pledging themselves* to human wolves and bears that they would not interfere to rescue them, and would not suffer others to do it. Oh, ye degenerate sons of the immortal Wesley! how shall ye escape the condemnation of outraged Christianity and civilization? The future historian of the Methodist Episcopal Church will blush with shame when he comes to the proceedings of this annual session of your Conference."—(*Pictures of Slavery*, pp. 282, 283.)

Let the reader compare these "anti-slavery" resolutions with the resolutions passed by the Conference held in that same city seventy-seven years before, as already quoted on page 17, and see if the "anti-slavery" of that region in 1857 is the same that "the fathers" inculcated there in 1780. That the contrast may be the more palpable, we place the old and new resolutions side by side in parallel columns:

"*Quest.* 17. Does this Conference acknowledge that slavery is contrary to the laws of God, man, and nature, and hurtful to society; contrary to the dictates of conscience and pure religion, and doing that we would not others should do to us and ours? Do we pass our disapprobation on all our friends who keep slaves, and advise their freedom?

"*Ans.* Yes."—(*Min's*, v. i. p. 12.)

"*Resolved*, By the Baltimore Conference, in Conference assembled, that we highly deprecate the agitation of the slavery question, which has already resulted to the great detriment of the political and religious interests of the country.

"*Resolved*, That, as heretofore, we will oppose with zeal any aggression which shall be attempted by the abolition agitations of the country."

Alas for Methodism! alas for humanity! alas for Christianity and justice! when the career of the most spiritual and evangelical Church in the land is marked by an apostasy so terrible, and a blindness and callousness so loudly calling for the judgments of Heaven upon us! Who can contemplate it and not exclaim—"Surely judgment is turned away backward, and justice standeth afar off; for truth is fallen in the street, and equity cannot enter. Yea, truth faileth; and he that departeth from evil maketh himself a prey."* How signally is this last remark verified in the cases of Revs. LONG, and MCCARTER, and CUNNINGHAM, and LAME, and many others, who, the moment they take a decided stand against oppression, are maligned in every possible way, and made a "prey" to every species of detraction! So it was with Wilberforce and Clarkson in England, and with the active abolitionists from 1840 to 1844 in our own Church; and so it will be until the battle is fought, the victory won, and the trump of Jubilee, filled with the breath of the Almighty, shall proclaim from every tower and bulwark and palace of our beloved Church, that SLAVERY in her bosom shall be no longer!

"They that will live godly in Christ Jesus shall suffer persecution." And so in the struggle with slavery. It is our solemn conviction, that a man who is not *decided* enough, and *active* enough, and *fearless* enough to offend the slave interest of the South, and their apologists at the North, and be well abused on that account, will never do much harm to the cause of slavery. He is too much like a Christian who serves God so "prudently" as never to offend Satan, or materially to disturb his sway in the earth. But we must close this chapter.

At the time of the separation in 1845, most of the slaveholders seceded; but the Baltimore Conference, being partly in slave territory and partly on free soil, did not go with the seceders. For this there were several reasons. In defending their own action in the case of Mr. Harding, they had offended the Southern fire-eaters and conciliated the North; and, moreover, they were not then as pro-slavery as other portions of the South. They staid with the North, therefore, and by this means considerable slave territory, and not a few slaveholders, were still left within the present bounds of the Methodist Episcopal Church. And so further west, in Western Virginia,

* Isaiah, lix. 14, 15.

Kentucky, Missouri, and Arkansas, we had slave territory left under our jurisdiction, and more or less slaveholders. Of the effects of this leaven of iniquity still left in the Church, the reader will learn more in the next chapter.

CHAPTER III.

OUR PRESENT CONNECTION WITH SLAVERY.—SLAVEHOLDERS IN THE PRIVATE MEMBERSHIP.

In this chapter we shall show that we have now from ten to twenty thousand slaveholders among the private members of the Methodist Episcopal Church.

The present Methodist Episcopal Church in these United States consists of 47 annual conferences; 6502 travelling preachers; 7530 local preachers; and 956,555 members and probationers.* Of these, about 600 travelling preachers, 800 local preachers, and 100,000 members are in slave territory—in Delaware, Maryland, Virginia, Kentucky, Missouri, and Arkansas. This is "the infected district"—the part of the body spiritual upon which the gangrene of slavery still lingers; and in this chapter we propose to show, that notwithstanding the stampede of slaveholders in 1845, *we are now, as a Church, more deeply and criminally involved in slaveholding than at any former period of our history.* For this there have been several causes, some of which we will here enumerate.

1. A border of slave territory was left in the Methodist Episcopal Church after the secession. Many of the preachers and members in Delaware, Maryland, Virginia, Kentucky, Missouri, and Arkansas, still adhered to the North, among whom were thousands of slaveholders in the private membership, and not a few in the local ministry.

2. The great issue raised with the "Methodist Episcopal Church South," after the secession, diverted the mind of the North from the subject of the remaining Methodist slaveholding on the border.

---

* General Minutes for 1858.

3. The Wesleyan secession of 1843 had taken many of the most earnest anti-slavery men, both lay and clerical, out of the Methodist Episcopal Church.

4. The stand taken by the Baltimore Conference in the case of Bishop Andrew, though it was no indication of anti-slavery principle, secured for a time the confidence of the North, and led to special care not to press them too hard upon the subject of slavery, and to regard them with sympathy and forbearance.

5. The oft-repeated and solemn declarations of the representatives of the Border Conferences, Baltimore especially, that there was little slaveholding within their territory; that what existed there was of the most mild and benevolent type; and that Methodism was fast loosening the chains of the slave, and reducing the amount of slaveholding;—this testimony from men who ought to be worthy of credit, led the Church to forego its inquiries and scrutiny as to the amount and quality of slaveholding within her pale, and the result will soon appear. Even as late as the last General Conference, we were assured that there was but little slavery in the Church, and that if let alone there would soon be none. So emphatically was this old story repeated, that the Committee on the Pastoral Address reported, and the General Conference adopted, the statement that "LITTLE OR NO MERCENARY SLAVEHOLDING EXISTS IN THE CHURCH."—(*Journal*, vol. iii. p. 297.) Thus the Church has been rocked to sleep; while the enemy has sowed his tares, till we are now far worse off, so far as slavery is concerned, than we were when the Wesleyans seceded in 1843: or at the time of the great Southern secession in 1844. This will be abundantly apparent as we proceed to establish the proposition that *we have now from ten to twenty thousand lay slaveholders in the Church;* and to the chapters which follow.

I. In their Episcopal Address for 1856, our bishops said:

"We have six Annual Conferences which are wholly or in part in slave territory. These Conferences have a white Church membership, including probationers, of more than one hundred and forty-three thousand. * * * They have a colored Church membership, including probationers, of more than twenty-eight thousand," &c.—(*Journals*, vol. iii. p. 199.)

But they included the whole of the Philadelphia and Baltimore Conferences, which are only in part in slave territory; and from careful estimates we are satisfied that our membership in slave territory does not exceed one hundred thousand.

Of these we believe that at least *fifteen thousand* are slaveholders!

II. Great numbers of colored people are held as slaves within the territory of the Methodist Episcopal Church.

The slave territory still covered by our Church, exclusive of Texas, amounts to about 231,914 square miles, viz.:

	sq. miles.		sq. miles.
Delaware	2,120	Kentucky	37,680
Maryland	11,124	Missouri	67,380
Virginia	61,352*	Arkansas	52,198
District of Columbia	60		
		Total	231,914

In this territory there are 3,237,458 whites, 914,376 slaves, 136,958 slaveholders, and about 100,000 Methodists: as the following from the census of 1850, will show:

States.	Whites.	Slaves.	Slaveholders.	Methodists.
Delaware	71,169	2,290	809	90,000†
Maryland	717,943	90,368	16,040	
Virginia	894,800	472,528	55,063	
Dist. of Columbia	37,940	3,687	1,477	
Kentucky	761,413	210,981	38,385	3,048
Missouri	592,004	87,422	19,185	6,270
Arkansas	162,189	47,100	5,999	1,262
	3,237,458	914,376	136,958	100,580

The proportion of white males over twenty years of age is about one fifth; so that the proportion of 3,237,458 who are over *twenty-one* years of age, and therefore capable of owning slaves, cannot exceed 650,000. Among these there are 136,958 slaveholders, or about one out of every five. If then the 50,000 male Methodists in this border territory, as a whole, hold slaves in the same proportion that others do, there are at least 10,000 slaveholders among these 100,580 Methodists.

But even this is not a fair estimate. It is well known that the most wealthy class own the slaves in all the slave States; and it is equally well known that the Methodists of Delaware, Maryland, and Virginia, are the wealthiest class in the community. The just inference therefore is, that the Methodists there hold even more than an average proportion of the slaves.

* A slight deduction should be made here for Southern Virginia, but as the conclusion is reached by the *ratio* of slaveholders, &c., it in nowise effects the result.

† This amount is estimated for those portions of the Baltimore and Philadelphia Conferences lying in slave territory. The balance is from the Minutes of 1858.

Somebody in these States holds nearly a million of human beings in bondage—one fourth of all the slaves in the United States—and the fair presumption is, that inasmuch as the Discipline does not forbid it, the Methodists there own their full share of them. And this presumption is strengthened by the opinions of those who have lived in those States, and know the amount of slaveholding there by our members.

III. Some time in 1852, or 1853, we think, a slave escaped from his Methodist master, and fled into Pennsylvania. His master pursued him; the slave armed himself and resisted, and finally the pursuing master, whose name was Gorsuch, we believe, was shot and killed. Not long after, a flaming obituary of this Methodist man-stealer was published in the *Christian Advocate and Journal*, the great official organ of the Church, expressing much sympathy for the "unfortunate" oppressor, but without an intimation of disapproval of the infamous business in which he lost his life. We write wholly from memory, but presume most of our readers will recollect the circumstances.

IV. Dr. I. T. Cooper, of the Philadelphia Conference, and a strong opposer of the abolitionists, declares that to such an extent are the male members of the Church in Maryland slaveholders, that the Official Boards could not be organized without taking such for leaders, stewards, &c.* Now there are some 100,000 members in that region, say 50,000 males. Ten officers to every hundred members is a large officiary, which would require only 5000 to fill the offices; and yet Dr. Cooper informs us that these offices cannot be filled by non-slaveholders. There are not enough of them! If the doctor's excuse for trampling upon the "Discipline as it is," is founded in truth (which we cannot doubt), then have we, at least, 30,000 instead of 10,000 slaveholders in Maryland and Virginia alone. Only think of it! Of 50,000 male members in this part of our Church territory, not enough are *not* slaveholders to man the Official Boards!

V. Rev. J. D. Long, in his "Pictures of Slavery in Church and State," declares that our members in Maryland and Virginia are deeply involved in slaveholding.

---

* Articles in the *Christian Advocate and Journal.*

Brother Long is now, and has been for some twenty years, a worthy member of the Philadelphia Conference. He was born in Maryland; his father was a slaveholder, and he himself became the owner of a slave on the death of his father. But he manumitted him at once for Christ's sake; and recently, against every earthly interest, except the pleasure of doing right, has borne his solemn testimony against the sum of all villanies. For this he has been maligned and persecuted in almost every possible way;* till at length he was obliged to flee, like a hunted roe, from the land of his birth and the grave of his father, to find a refuge and a home on the free soil of the North.† We know Brother Long personally, and we venture the assertion, not only that prior to his recent disclosures, he was one of the last men in all his Conference whose word anybody would call in question; but that no candid person can see and talk with him for an hour, without being satisfied of his entire truthfulness and moral honesty. And now what says Brother Long? Hear him!

"According to the minutes of the Conference,‡ in 1856, there were upwards of 15,000 white members and probationers in the slave portion of the Conference. Of this number there are at least 1000 mercenary slaveholders;§ these thousand slaveholders own at least 3000 slaves. Numbers own from five to ten. I know one individual who owns twenty. Intelligent laymen, in that section of the country, will not think this a large estimate, but quite within the bounds of truth.

"I cannot speak for the Baltimore Conference, though it is certain that it has a vastly larger slaveholding territory than the Philadelphia Conference. If that Conference has jurisdiction over one thousand mercenary slaveholders, and these own 3000 slaves, then we have 6000 slaves owned by 2000 members of the Methodist Episcopal Church, all sheltered by the Discipline of our Church.

"It is my opinion that 8000 of our Philadelphia Conference members, who are not actual slaveholders, are yet advocates of slavery; and would rejoice to inherit slaves, or otherwise obtain them. If these 3000 or 6000 slaves, doomed in their persons and posterity to toil that others may reap, could have appeared before the General Conference of 1856, that noble and generous body of Christian ministers would have been moved to tears. Indeed, the poor slave cannot go to Conventions and Conferences to plead his own cause. He cannot know his benefactors. His mind is doomed to eternal barrenness. He who advocates his cause, in the public estimation, par-

* We have before us a letter sent to him from Maryland, containing a quantity of negroes' hair filled with Scotch snuff. These, we suppose, are plantation logic—the black wool to stop the ears of Mercy, and snuff to blind the eyes of Justice, to the slashed and bleeding bodies, and the screams and entreaties of tortured slaves.

† Brother Long is now settled at Auburn, N. Y.

‡ The Philadelphia, which takes in but a small portion of the slave territory under examination.

§ This does not include all, of course.

takes in some degree of his degradation. I will advance another opinion. I do it with caution. I know it will be called in question, if not positively denied; but I court investigation; and if the statement can be proved false, I will rejoice.

"I make bold to declare that there are more slaves owned *now* by members of the Methodist Episcopal Church than in 1845," &c.—(*Pictures*, p. 49.)

In this estimate, Brother Long does not pretend to include all who hold slaves; for he says:

"By actual slaveholders, I mean those who hold them for gain, just as the utterly irreligious do; without any reference to brethren who have manumitted their slaves, to be free at twenty-five, thirty, or thirty-five years."—(*Ibid.*)

Again: "At one small county appointment," says Brother Long, "in the fall of 1855 and winter of 1856, I knew two members of the Methodist Episcopal Church who died and left from twenty-five to thirty slaves in bondage for life."* In another place he says:

"Within the last seven years, a member of the Methodist Episcopal Church, of the highest standing, made a will, by which he left his slaves to be sold at auction to the highest bidder, the money to be invested for the use of his family. After his death, the will was carried out to the letter. This act was regarded as a shrewd business transaction by the community in which he had lived, and was not thought to reflect in the slightest degree on his Christian character. The newspapers eulogized his virtues in extravagant language."—(Page 385.)

Such then is the testimony of this unimpeached and unimpeachable witness, who has lived in the midst of slavery, and knows whereof he affirms; and of whose motives for telling the truth it may be said, as one said of the Apostles,

Unask'd their pains, ungrateful their advice,
Starving their gains, and martyrdom their price.

VI. Rev. J. M. McCarter, another member of the Philadelphia Conference, is our next witness. Brother M. is now (1858) stationed at Reading, Pa., and is both an able and worthy minister, and an excellent writer. In his startling pamphlet, "*Border Methodism and Border Slavery*," he says:

"*Many of our private members are slaveholders.* We do not say that these are numerous when compared with the thousands of members in Maryland and Virginia, and Sussex county, Delaware. We have given some attention to the question, and from our observation on the two districts, Easton and Snow Hill, we have come to the conclusion, that there are about fifteen hundred members of our Church in the Philadelphia Annual Conference

---

* *Pictures*, p. 34.

who are slaveholders. We give five hundred to Easton and one thousand to Snow Hill District. These, we think, are owners of about 4000 slaves. This is not too large an estimate. It has been made up and the figures obtained from those ministers who have spent a large part of the last ten years on those districts. My own observation would lead me to regard the number above given as probably correct. * * * * The proportion of slaveholders to the entire membership (white) on Snow Hill District is about one to every ten; on Easton District, one to every seventeen."—(Page 21.)

This estimate, it must be remembered, is only for *two districts*, in the Philadelphia Conference; leaving the whole of the Baltimore, Kentucky, Missouri, and Arkansas Conferences out of the account.

VII. Rev. J. S. LAME, another member of the Philadelphia Conference, who has lived in "the infected district," fully confirms the statements of Brothers Long and McCarter, as to the amount of slaveholding in this border region. In his pamphlet just published, "*Maryland Slavery and Maryland Chivalry*,"* Brother Lame says:

"Such were the abominations of the traffic, as practised by Church members and ministers, by professors and publicans, that we were driven to the admission that, considering the circumstances, the American is the worst system of slavery that ever saw the sun; and, with our eye fixed on the fires of the last judgment, we aver that such shocking abomination, grinding oppression, cruel barbarities, unrelenting despotism, and foul impurities, are practised on the Eastern Shore of Maryland, as would have disgraced earth's most barbarous age and nation. And yet the system, with which these atrocities seem inseparably connected, finds apologists innumerable in the Church, and even among God's ministers."—(Page 6.)

Take, also, the following additional extracts from the same work, as illustrating both the *amount* and the *character* of the Methodist slaveholding in the Philadelphia Conference. Don't fail to read it because it is in fine print:

"A little more than a twelvemonth since, a member of the Methodist Episcopal Church died, having left a slave, whom another Methodist sold to a 'nigger-buyer.' Another died within a shorter period of time, and his two-legged cattle were sold along with his four-legged. A Methodist owned a slave girl that was receiving the attention of a colored man: he worked hard, lived economically, and bought this girl for a wife; he took a bill of sale, and filed a deed of manumission the same day. That slave never cost that Methodist master one cent; he got her by inheritance; her splendid moral, spiritual, and literary education devolved upon the shoulders of others; for, be it understood, that she graduated with distinguished honors at the most eminent literary institution for the people of color south of Mason

* This title does not sufficiently indicate the character of the work. It should rather be called, "*Further Light upon Border Methodism and Border Slavery*," as that is its real character.

and Dixon's Line (her *alma mater* was the kitchen!), yet when this honorable, high-minded negro man wanted a companion, he had to pay hundreds of dollars to a Methodist master for her."—(Pages 31, 32.)

"A devoted Methodist, recently in the presence of the writer, was dilating upon the thorough and efficacious cowhiding he had given his black woman, for refusing patiently to submit to a thrashing from her indignant mistress! While listening to the recital, my blood boiled a little, but suddenly cooled down lower than zero, upon recollecting that our Church is 'conservative,' and that 'agitation is much to be deplored,' it being peculiary offensive to doctors."—(Page 29.)

"In one of the epistles of 'Junius,' a Methodist master is spoken of who 'boasted of the thorough and efficacious cowhiding he had administered to his slave women.' This good brother, becoming provoked at the misconduct of one of his colored women, beat and stamped her to that degree, that medical aid was requisite to preserve life and restore health. It seems that the flagellation of females is of frequent occurrence on the Eastern Shore; for another brother stoutly maintained that 'Junius' meant him, for it was his case described. We learned that this brother employed a broom-handle for a rod of correction. And still another brother complained that 'Junius' had given to the public the fact that he had cudgelled his black women; but gave the assurance that the whipping was deserved. Now we have to tell all these dear brethren, 'Junius' meant neither. It was a Methodist in another county to which he alluded."—(Page 49.)

"On one occasion the narrator was at the house of the master, when some chickens were missing. The theft was attributed to a certain slave. He was called up, and denied the charge; but, as the narrator was leaving the farm, he heard the sound of heavy blows, and the voice of the slave crying: 'O my God, massa!' But no helping hand was nigh to deliver him. The slave who was at the wedding attempted to abscond; he got as far as the lower portion of the State of Delaware, and was apprehended. His master placed one end of a rope around his neck, and fastened the other to his carriage, and thus brought him home in hot haste."—(Page 10.)

"We have seen sights, and heard sounds, that might make the cheeks of a devil blush for his honor. We have seen the child of three summers torn from its mother's convulsive grasp, where her groans might almost be heard by the minister in the Methodist Episcopal sanctuary. We have seen the panting fugitive dragged back to his hated task. We have seen the ministers of Christ offer their reward for the return of runaways; and we have known one to spend the sacred Sabbath in getting the dogs of the law to fasten their fangs in the flesh of his brother—(one of his own color). We have seen the wife violently separated from the husband; and the children separated from the mother. These are the natural and inevitable product of the system of slavery—a system that finds a thousand apologists."—(Page 56.)

"Their magnificent, may I not say princely entertainment, for a fortnight, consisted of one peck of unsifted corn-meal, ten pounds of pork, or rather rancid bacon, and one quart of molasses. Often have I seen those negroes, property, too, of that wealthy Methodist, work in the sultry sun till twelve o'clock at noon, and then come to the kitchen to mix and cook their chicken feed for dinner, and on bended knees, from my wife would beg a little salt." —(Page 14.)

"A slave, belonging to a Methodist of extensive wealth, waited on the writer, and designated an evening on which he wished to be married, and brought with him, as is usual in such cases, a certificate from the master, which we insert:

"'Mr. Lane you may marry my man John to my girl An. i give my concent. (Signed) J. S.'

"We told *plain* John that he ought to ask '*massa* John' for a dollar to give the preacher for getting married; and John brought the munificent sum of twenty-five cents."—(Page 9.)

"For his first wife he married a slave belonging to ——; that —— sold his wife and a part of his children South. Said I, 'Why did you not marry a free girl?' 'I was guine to, massa, but massa told me he put me in his pocket (that is, sell him to the South), if I married a free girl.' "—(Page 18.)

By the laws of the Slave States, children follow the condition of the mother; hence, if the poor slave married a free woman, his children would be free. Hence the master compelled him to marry a slave, that he might enslave his children. Brother Lame proceeds:

"As to the statement [of Brother Long] of the number of slaves held by members of the Methodist Episcopal Church, I do not think it at all extravagant. A certain church, on a certain circuit, numbering only one hundred members, will furnish one sixtieth of that number; multiply every one hundred members in the slaveholding district by fifty, and see the product."—(Page 30.)

There are now over 18,000 white members in the Wilmington and Snow Hill districts; hence, if every one hundred held fifty slaves, there must be 9000 slaves held by Methodists in those two districts alone.

Speaking of a conversation with one of his stewards, Brother Lame says:

"It was there warmly maintained, by a circuit steward, that he did not pretend to hold his slaves for any other purpose whatsoever than a mercenary purpose, if by mercenary is meant for hire or gain; and he was utterly unable to understand the speech of Rev. J. A. Collins, delivered at the late General Conference, in which he asserted that there is little or no mercenary slaveholding in the Church."—(Page 29.)

The statement here alluded to, was in the Pastoral Address, and not in Mr. Collins' speech. Mr. C. had the frankness to say in private more than once, that the Methodists in the Baltimore Conference held their slaves for the same reason that others did, viz., because they wanted their work.

But to proceed with our extracts:

"One old, back-bent, hard-handed man of toil stated that, in his younger days, he labored all day for his master, and spent the whole of six consecutive nights working for his personal benefit; and that, when he expressed his wish to marry a free girl, his master, to intimidate him, threatened to sell him South. He married a slave, and, as a consequence, that wife, with a portion of his children, are now toiling under the burning sun of the South."—(Page 8.)

We close with the following illustration of the blessedness of being owned by a pious Methodist master:

"On one occasion, I found a little black girl employed as waiting-maid, in fact a general convenience. She seemed like an inoffensive, timid creature. A severe snow-storm arrived about the same time we did, and the weather was fearfully cold. 'Hett' must with dispatch execute all orders, whether issued by her master of forty, or her master of four years of age. Her wearing apparel consisted of two garments. Frequently have I seen her ankle deep in the snow, with neither shoes nor stockings on. Hett fell heir to all the supernumerary shoes of the family, great and small; and when, from long service to others, they became superannuated, it was her fortune to be destitute. Her suffering condition appealing to my sympathies, on condition of her performing a small job, I promised to purchase her a pair of shoes. But this proposition seemed to arouse the dormant humanity of his majesty, her liege lord, and he procured her a pair. Taking a walk unexpectedly on the lawn in the rear of the house, I found poor Hett 'getting it good,' as it is termed, with a large sized hoop-pole. I quietly returned, not having any special preference for such spectacles. One day Hett came to my room, to receive my orders as usual, when upon looking up I found a frightful gash in her cheek. Said I, 'What is the matter?' She hung her head, and refused to answer; but on being pressed, and assured that no danger would follow, she replied: 'Massa.' 'Where was it done?' 'In the barn.'

"I felt indignant that such a looking object should have been permitted to enter my room. A few mornings subsequently I saw barefooted Hett come from the barn with a bleeding face, followed by her master. As the kind-hearted brother approached, I inquired if it was he that had struck her in the face. 'Don't know,' was the answer. I replied, 'You ought to know.'

"Some time subsequently my soul was sickened at the sight of her forehead laid open for an inch and a half in length, and penetrating to the skull. I determined to investigate the matter, and found that a whipping was the cause of the wound, and not by the lash. Her gracious master, attempting to chastise her while standing on the ice, she, in an effort to dodge the blow, fell and struck her head. * * * * Poor Hett! I have devoutly prayed that she might soon die, for death can be her only deliverance."—(Pages 15, 16.)

Such is the testimony of Brother LAME, a member of the Philadelphia Conference, who has lived in the midst of our border Methodism and slavery, and *knows* whereof he affirms. And yet we have professed anti-slavery ministers among us, even at the North, who think we have but little slaveholding in our Church on the border, and that of a very mild and anti-slavery type! Oh, for some potent eye-salve, that they may see and believe!

VIII. Rev. H. C. ATWATER, of the Providence Conference, now stationed at South Manchester, Connecticut, made a tour through four of the Border Conferences to ascertain, by personal observation, the true connection of our Church there with slavery; and in an article in *Zion's Herald* for October 21, 1857, he gives us the results of his observation. Though the article is somewhat long to copy entire, we conclude to lay it before our readers, as it affords the best possible testimony upon the point in hand, and is richly worth perusal.

Dr. HAVEN had just before been eulogizing the Missouri and Arkansas Methodists as "anti-slavery," to which Brother Atwater thus triumphantly replies:

"POSITION OF OUR BORDER BRETHREN ON THE SUBJECT OF SLAVERY.

"MR. EDITOR:—Will you allow a word of correction in respect to one or two sentences of an editorial headed 'Our Southwestern Border,' in the *Herald* of September 16th? I feel assured you wish to state the truth, and would not have made those statements if you had been personally acquainted with the facts in the case. Speaking of the objections many have to the appropriation of missionary money to build up pro-slavery churches in the Border Conferences, you say: 'Our Church is there decidedly an anti-slavery Church.' Again, 'Our Church is the great anti-slavery vanguard in those States.' I wish it were even so; then would there be hope for our Church and our country. But nothing is further from the truth.

"Some months since I resolved to ascertain personally the facts in the case. I travelled extensively in Missouri, Arkansas, Kentucky, and Virginia, and the result of that thorough examination was, that I found no Methodists more intensely pro-slavery in Alabama, Louisiana, or in any of the 'fire-eating' parts of the South, than I found the members of our mission churches to be in the Border Conferences; they utterly abjure the name of abolitionists, or of having any sympathy with the anti-slavery movements in the free States. It matters not how many slaves a man owns, it is no objection to his becoming a member of those mission churches. It is true, as you set forth in that article, that the Church South charge the members of our Church in the Missouri, Arkansas, and Kentucky Conferences with belonging to an anti-slavery body. And now, if our membership there could or would admit the truthfulness of the charge, and reply, 'What you think our disgrace, we consider our *highest glory*, and are ready to acknowledge that we intend to labor in all proper ways for the freedom of the slave,' I should be in favor of pouring out our money like water to sustain them. I wish there was some proof that they are the vanguard of freedom's army; but, alas! on the contrary, they most unequivocally and categorically deny the charge that any anti-slavery blood is in their veins, or that any action of the General Conference can be pointed out to prove that the Church North is abolitionized. They tell them, truthfully, that the division of 1844 did not turn on the hinge of the sin of slavery, but on the minor and non-essential point, whether a bishop might hold slaves or not. They remind them of the thousands of slaves held without a word of rebuke by the membership, in six of the Conferences of the Northern Church; that travelling preachers even, in those Conferences, can have their houses filled up with slaves, have all the avails of slave-labor, if the wife's father, or some convenient friend, only holds the title-deed. They quote to their Southern calumniators, as perfect extinguishers, the hair-spun and sophistical arguments of those who are wearing out life in the *honorable work* (?) of showing that slavery is 'constitutionally' in the Church, and encompassed and defended with brazen armor. And I am only sorry to say, that the pro-slavery course of the Church North furnishes them with abundance of material to silence those who accuse them of belonging to an anti-slavery Church.

"The position of the Northern and Southern Methodist Episcopal Churches in the disputed territory may be somewhat illustrated by reference to the Old and New School Presbyterian Churches in the South; they are crowding and jostling, each trying to obtain the advantage of the other, filling the community with bitterness and sectarianism, while both are there heartily pro-slavey. The points upon which they differ are so trivial, that they ought never to be mentioned among Christian brethren.

"The result with them and with us is this, that party spirit, aided by missionary money from those who sympathize with either side, keeps two small churches in existence, where it would be far better for the quiet and religious welfare of the community if there was but one.

"The American Home Missionary Society has adopted a most salutary rule, which works well for the cause of humanity, viz., that they will grant funds to no Church that allows slaveholders among its members. We must adopt the same, if we would have our missionary treasury full; it is too late in the day to suppose that anti-slavery men will contribute money to build up pro-slavery churches. The patrons of the Missionary Society have a *right to know how their money is expended.*

"This question is now before the churches, and must be met without any dodging. Let those who have any personal knowledge of the anti or pro slavery character of the churches assisted by the missionary money in the Border Conferences, bring it forward. H. C. ATWATER."

In commenting upon this letter, in the same paper, Dr. Haven said:

"Now we place implicit confidence in his testimony based on actual observation. There never was a grosser mistake—to call it by no graver name—than that insisted upon at the last General Conference, and repeated earnestly since, that mercenary slaveholding does not exist undisturbed in *some* of the societies connected with the Methodist Episcopal Church. This fact is asserted by Rev. J. D. Long, and others who must know. It is asserted by our correspondent from actual observation. It is asserted, too, by a whole class of witnesses, consisting of ministers of the Methodist Episcopal Church South, whom, of course, our friends on the Border will and must allow to be good witnesses, since they interchange pulpits with them, and invite them to preach at our camp-meetings, and to dedicate our churches to Almighty God."

Such seem to have been the views of Dr. Haven a year ago, though lately he seems to have concluded, despite the testimony of Brother Atwater and others whom he named in this article, that the far western border, at least, is decidedly anti-slavery! He "don't believe a word" of the statement that they are otherwise!! We regret this seeming vacillation on the part of the *Herald*, but hope, after it has swung like a pendulum to the other extreme, it will come back to the above faith again before 1860.

Desiring to obtain the most reliable information from original sources, we addressed a letter of inquiry to Rev. Brother Atwater, and since the above was written have received the following answer, which we commend to the reader's especial attention:

"South Manchester, Ct., *October* 6, 1858.

"Dear Brother M.:—I am the person you refer to in your note of inquiry. * * * * Ever since the formation of those missionary Border Conferences in slave territory, our Conference has been assured by those managing the missionary money in New York, that it was for our highest interest, as anti-slavery men, to keep those missionaries there—that they were laboring most efficiently for the overthrow of slavery, &c.

"Knowing that those Conferences were established by the pro-slavery party in the Church, to strengthen their interest, and that the men laboring there had been taken from *strong*, not to say *rabid* pro-slavery Conferences, I had reason to doubt whether they were doing efficient service in the anti-slavery cause.

"I therefore gave six months of time and money to the examination of the Border work, and the region beyond. Travelling in Missouri, Arkansas, Kentucky, Tennessee, and Virginia, as well as in the States bordering on the Mexican Gulf—so that I can probably say, without egotism, that I am better posted with facts in regard to the number of slaves held in the Border Conferences, as a whole, and of the strength of the slaveholding spirit among preachers and people there, than any other person in the Church North.

"Among many things learned in that examination, the following *facts were fully demonstrated:*

"*First*, That the Methodist Episcopal Church North, in the slaveholding States and in the mission Conferences referred to, both as to ministers and members, were *as strongly pro-slavery as the Methodist Episcopal Church South.* Both, with equal sensitiveness, repudiated the idea of being abolitionists, or of having any sympathy with an abolition Church, or of desiring to have the slaves enjoy liberty.

"*Secondly*, The fact of owning slaves, of living on the toil of unrequited labor, is not the slightest bar to membership in any of our mission churches.

"*Thirdly*, That it is a great and uncalled-for waste of missionary money to keep men in those Mission or Border Conferences, preaching an emasculated Gospel, silent upon one of the greatest sins upon which the sun shines; building up pro-slavery churches to head off the spirit of anti-slavery, which has become so strong that it threatens to give this monster sin no longer a baptized place in the Church. The heathen are calling in vain for the word of God, while thousands of money are turned aside to *cherish and make strong* the pro-slavery interest in the Church.

"*Fourthly*, Should a census be taken by our Church of the number of slaves held by her members (as there ought to be, and which could be done with little trouble), it would greatly astonish those who, without having examined this subject personally, honestly believe that the instances of slaveholding are very rare among our members.

"Sympathizing with you in behalf of the oppressed, and earnestly desiring that our sacred missionary money may no longer be turned aside from promulgating a *free Gospel* to aid one that is bound, and offers chains to the colored man—I remain fraternally yours,

"H. C. Atwater."

One would very naturally conclude from the drift of this letter, that we had inquired with special reference to our southwestern Mission Conferences. But this was not the case. Our inquiry related to the letter in the *Herald*, already inserted on p. 51, and to the general subject of Methodist slaveholding on the Border. And such is the testimony of this most competent and reliable witness.

IX. Arthur Hughes, Esq., of Syracuse, N. Y., was in Jefferson City, Missouri, a year ago last August. While there, he stopped at the house of a Methodist lady. One morning he heard the slashings of a horsewhip, and a terrible outcry from a young female slave, and on going to the window saw this Methodist sister whipping her slave most unmercifully. The *crime* for which she was thus brutally scourged was this: the slave had a little boy, a mulatto, whose every feature and action proclaimed him the grandchild of this Methodist slaveholder; and in washing the little fellow, his slave mother had used a little more water (which had to be drawn from the river) than her mistress thought she ought to; and then came the lash. And what is still worse, this slaveholding, slave-whipping mother in Israel—this model Missouri Methodist—boasted of having been for thirty-seven years a member of the Methodist Episcopal Church; and, like the slaveholding Dr. Deems, at that very time professed to enjoy the blessing of entire sanctification!

Brother Hughes is a worthy citizen of Syracuse, upon whose testimony any jury would hang any Methodist preacher in America, if he had committed a capital offence; and such is his positive knowledge of the "anti-slavery" character of Missouri Methodism, in one instance at least. Nor will it be a sufficient answer for some brother in Kansas or in St. Louis to say, "*we* don't know of any such Methodism." What if they don't know of it? Others do, and their testimony is positive and unimpeachable. Slaveholding Missouri Methodism is like the same kind of Methodism of all other States,—corrupt as Sodom, and cruel as the grave.

X. That slaveholding is largely practised by our membership on the Border Conferences may be inferred from the following significant facts:

(1.) A motion was made at the last General Conference to

change the General Rule on slavery, so that it should forbid "the buying, selling, or holding a human being as property." When the vote was taken on this proposition, all the delegates from the slaveholding Conferences voted *against* it. Of the thirty-three delegates from the Philadelphia, Baltimore, Western Virginia, Kentucky, Missouri, and Arkansas Conferences, none were absent, and not a vote was lost. They voted "*solid*" against any change, thus showing that for *some* reason they did not wish to prohibit slaveholding in the Methodist Episcopal Church.—(See *Journal for* 1856, p. 127.)

(2.) At a later period in the Conference, a motion was made as follows:

"*Resolved*, That the Book Agents and Tract Secretary be, and they hereby are, instructed to publish, in tract or book form, such anti-slavery matter as the subject of slavery may demand, including Mr. Wesley's Thoughts on Slavery."

On this question, all the above delegates first voted to postpone action indefinitely; and when that failed, all voted *against the resolution*. This shows us precisely *what kind* of "anti-slavery" our ministers inculcate in Maryland, Virginia, Missouri, &c.; and what the probabilities are as to the amount of slaveholding in the Border Conferences.

XI. Apart from all other testimony, it is matter of public notoriety on our *Northern* border, that a large proportion of the slaves who run away are the "property" of professed Methodist masters. We have conversed with many, on their way to a land of freedom, and we give it as our deliberate opinion that *three fourths* of all the fugitives who pass over the eastern branch of the underground railroad, run away from Methodist masters in Maryland and Virginia—from the Gorsuches and Harpers and Pattisons and Traverses of Border Methodism.

Such are the evidences upon which we base our belief that we have now from ten to twenty thousand lay and unofficial slaveholders in the Methodist Episcopal Church. And yet, with all these facts existing, whether known to any Northern delegates or not, the last General Conference were so misled by the Border delegates, or something else, as to declare, in their Pastoral Address, that "LITTLE OR NO MERCENARY SLAVEHOLDING EXISTS IN THE CHURCH!"*

* Printed Journal, p. 297.

CHAPTER IV.

SLAVEHOLDING OFFICIAL MEMBERS, LEADERS, STEWARDS, TRUSTEES, &c.

LET us next inquire to what extent slaveholding has come to be practised by official members, such as class-leaders, stewards, trustees, and exhorters, in the Border Conferences.

Though the Discipline nowhere prohibits slaveholding in the private membership, it does expressly forbid it in official members. It declares, page 212, that "no slaveholder shall be eligible to any official station in our Church hereafter, where the laws of the State in which he lives will admit of emancipation,* and permit the liberated slave to enjoy freedom." Now the laws of Maryland, Virginia, Delaware, the District of Columbia, Kentucky, Missouri, and Arkansas, all "admit of emancipation, and allow the liberated slave to enjoy freedom." There were in those States and the District, in 1850, according to the census, no less than 170,409 free people of color: viz., in the District of Columbia, 10,050; in Delaware, 18,073; in Maryland, 74,723; in Virginia, 54,333; in Kentucky, 10,011; in Missouri, 2611; and in Arkansas, 608. The laws of all this "Border" do therefore admit of emancipation, and over all the territory a slaveholder is ineligible to any ecclesiastical office by the long-established law of the Church. But how is this law regarded?

I. DR. I. T. COOPER, already referred to, in his defence of the administration on the Border, admits that a large portion of the officers of the Church there, leaders, trustees, stewards, &c., are slaveholders. His excuse is, that there are so few who do not hold slaves, that they could not get enough of such to constitute the official boards!

* It should be distinctly understood, in considering these cases, and those of the local and travelling preachers that follow, that the laws of *all* the States in which we have slaveholding members, allow of emancipation to the fullest extent. They are not restrained, therefore, by the laws of the land. But an effort is being made in Maryland, we believe, to secure a law forbidding all emancipation; and we have great reason to fear that our membership there are helping on the project. With *such* a law, leaders and stewards, local preachers, preachers in charge, and presiding elders, could all hold slaves without a breach of our present Lower Law Discipline. We hope, therefore, it will be keyed up at this point by the next General Conference, and placed a little above the slave laws of Maryland.

II. Br. Long repeatedly declares that no attention is paid to the Discipline upon this point—that stewards, leaders, and trustees hold slaves with impunity. In a letter to the N. C. *Advocate*, some months since, he says:

"Chattel slavery still exists in the Methodist Episcopal Church in the States of Delaware, Maryland, and Virginia. The *practical and administrative example and influence* of the Church in those States is to perpetuate and extend slavery, as far as the Philadelphia Conference of the Methodist Episcopal Church is concerned. I will name some of the circuits within the slaveholding portion of our Conference: Smyrna, Denton, Talbot, Easton, Centreville, Kent Island, Sudlersville, Kent, Millington, Seaford, Federalsburg, Dorchester, Church Creek, Cambridge, Blackwater, Quantico, Salisbury, Princess Anne, Annamessex, Accomac, Northampton, New Town, Snow Hill, Berlin, Worcester, Lewis, and Georgetown. I give it as my *opinion* that one half the number of all the trustees, class-leaders, exhorters, stewards, and local preachers on these circuits are slaveholders."

III. Br. McCarter bears testimony upon the same point. He says:

"*Many* of the stewards are slaveholders. To a great extent this office is represented by the moneyed men in the Church—the large holders of property. One half of the whole number of stewards on those districts are probably slaveholders. While on the upper portions of Maryland and in Delaware they are comparatively but as one in five, on the southern portions of both districts the precise reverse may be taken as the ratio. One half of the trustees of churches are probably connected with slavery. Exhorters, leaders, and local preachers are slaveholders."—(Page 21.)

IV. Brother Lame, who is also well acquainted with the facts, so far as the southern part of the Philadelphia Conference is concerned, and who has been driven from his circuit in Maryland within a year for writing certain anti-slavery articles for *Zion's Herald*, fully corroborates the statements of Brothers Long and McCarter upon this point. Indeed, most of the stewards who drove him off were slaveholders. Even one of the lay delegates at the last Philadelphia Conference—a Mr. Harper, we believe—was a slaveholder and a local preacher, a very suitable layman to sit with the slaveholding portion of the ministers.

In regard to slaveholding official members, Br. Lame says:

☞ "I have class-leaders, stewards, exhorters, local preachers, white and black, that hold slaves."—(Page 22.)

"Among the number [of slaves owned on his circuit] are twelve belonging to a circuit steward of the Methodist Episcopal Church."—(Page 24.)

"The Discipline certainly declares slaveholders ineligible to official station in the Church; but the members of the board of stewards owned at least thirty slaves, and bought, bred, beat, and sold them *ad libitum*. One member of that board we had frequently heard make the boastful assertion, that the moment his servants were dissatisfied and wished another master, they were at perfect liberty to go. So, taking the good brother at his own proposal, one night the whole *posse* took French leave; but no sooner was the fact known that they had gone, than a large reward was offered for their apprehension and recovery."—(Page 7.)

V. In November, 1857, twenty-eight fugitive slaves came up through Syracuse by the underground railroad, and passed on to Canada. At the same time the following advertisement appeared in the *Cambridge* (Md.) *Democrat* for Nov. 4, 1857:

$2,000 REWARD. Ran away from the subscriber, on Saturday night, 24th inst., fourteen head of negroes, viz.: 4 men, 2 women, one boy, and seven children. Kit is about 35 years of age, 5 feet 6 or 7 inches high. Joe is about 30 years old, very black, his teeth are very white, and is about 5 feet 8 inches high. Henry is about 22 years old, of dark chesnut color, and large front teeth. Joe is about 20 years old, heavy built, and black. Tom is about 16 years old, light chesnut color. Susan is about 35 years old, dark chesnut color, and rather stout built, speaks rather slow, and has with her 4 children, varying from 1 to 7 years old. Leah is about 28 years old, about 5 feet high, dark chesnut color, with 3 children, 2 boys and 1 girl, from 1 to 8 years old. I will give $1000 if taken in the county, $1500 if taken out of the county and in the State, and $2000 if taken out of the State; in either case to be lodged in Cambridge jail, so that I can get them again; or I will give a fair proportion of the above reward if any part are secured.

"SAMUEL PATTISON,
"*Oct.* 26, 1857. Near Cambridge, Md.

"P. S.—Since writing the above, I have discovered that my negro woman Sarah Jane, 25 years old, stout built, and chesnut color, has also run off. S. P."

Now this "Brother Pattison" is a member in high standing in the Methodist Episcopal Church in Dorchester county, Md., and a steward in the Church. What a gem of a Methodist he must be! How closely he has kept to the Discipline, and to the ancient landmarks as laid down by Wesley, and Clarke, and Watson, and Coke, and Asbury, and Garrettson, and McKendree! Shame on him, and upon all other such hypocrites and apostates from God and from original Methodism! It is enough to make the body of Wesley turn over in its grave to call such men Methodists. But we need not multiply proofs, illustrations, or comments under this head. The preceding are so clear and indubitable, that we should be likely to weaken rather than strengthen the impression by a further accumulation of testimony.

CHAPTER V.

SLAVEHOLDING LOCAL PREACHERS, DEACONS, AND ELDERS.

According to the general minutes for 1858, there are now in the six slaveholding Conferences 1012 local preachers, viz.: in

Two Baltimores	390	Kentucky	31
Philadelphia	338	Missouri	86
Western Virginia	176	Arkansas	29
		Total	1012

Allowing two hundred for those portions of the Philadelphia and Baltimore Conferences that are on free soil, we shall have 812 local preachers in slave territory, a large portion of whom we have reason to believe are slaveholders.

I. In his reply to the denial of Rev. F. G. Hibbard, Dr. Lee, of the *Richmond Christian Advocate*, asserts that "Local preachers and ordained ministers in the local ranks in the Methodist Episcopal Church North, are slaveholders." Notice, also, his declarations, copied at length in the next chapter.

II. Dr. M'Ferren, editor of the *Nashville Christian Advocate*, is equally full and explicit. In his printed letters to Bishop Morris, which have never been contradicted nor answered, he says:

> "You know that in Maryland and Virginia you have hundreds, yea, thousands of members who hold slaves; that you have ordained deacons and elders in the ministry of your Church, who are slaveholders. You yourself have ordained to the office and work of the ministry many a slaveholder. * * * Bishop Waugh, Bishop Morris, and Bishop Janes, to my certain knowledge, have each ordained slaveholders to the offices of deacon and elder."—*First letter to Bishop Morris.*

We suppose most of these cases were local preachers, and hence introduce the testimony here; but there are matters in the letter which will make it equally pertinent in the next chapter, where we shall introduce it again more at length, and with additional comments.

III. The celebrated memorial from the Westmoreland Circuit, Baltimore Conference, which was sent to the General Conference of 1840, represented "that local preachers within the jurisdiction of the Baltimore Conference, but residing in the commonwealth of Virginia, have, in considerable numbers, and for a succession of years, been rejected as applicants for deacons' and elders' orders in the ministry, solely on the ground of their being slaveholders, or the owners of slaves." * From this it is evident that at that time, and "for a succession of years," local preachers "in considerable numbers" were and had been slaveholders in Virginia. And it is not likely that it has grown any better since.

IV. Rev. Mr. Clemm, agent for the New Baltimore paper, stated on the floor of the last Philadelphia Conference, that the Baltimore Conference could not now prevent a slaveholding local preacher from being ordained, even if disposed to do so; and he presumed the Philadelphia Conference could not. To this statement no exceptions were taken. We understood the remark to imply that such was the state of public sentiment in that region, and the influence of slavery, that it would not do to refuse to ordain a man, simply because he was a slaveholder.

V. The following case in point was furnished for the *Northern Independent* in May last, by Rev. J. D. Long:

"The Rev. Henry Hutt, a free *colored* man residing on the Eastern Shore of Maryland, and *a local preacher* in the Philadelphia Annual Conference of the *Methodist Episcopal Church*, has, by the force of his talents and industry, accumulated considerable wealth. There is no proof that the Rev. Hutt is, or has ever been an abolitionist. He is a conservative, no doubt. It appears that some months ago a *slave owned* by the Rev. *Henry*, concluded to take the underground railroad for the land of the free, but failed, was caught, brought back to this Rev. *slaveholder*, was sold to the South, and the money pocketed by said Hutt. The Quarterly Conference did not take away his license for this conduct, and he is still a local preacher in our Church. Now, if said Henry had helped a man of his own color to run away from worse than Egyptian bondage, the Church would have branded him with disgrace, and the State sent him to the Penitentiary."

VI. Still another case in point will be found in the following advertisement, taken from the *Cambridge* (Md.) *Democrat.* Mark its modern date:

$300 REWARD. Ran away from the subscriber, from the neighborhood of Town Point, on Saturday night, 24th inst., my negro man, Aaron Cornish, about 35 years old. He is about 5 feet 10 inches high, black, good looking, rather pleasant countenance, and carries himself with a confident manner. He went off with his wife Daffney, a negro woman belonging to Rheuben E. Philips. I will give the above reward if taken out of the county, and $200 if taken in the county; in either case, to be lodged in Cambridge (Md.) jail.

Oct. 28, 1857. Levi D. Travers.

* Journal of General Conference for 1840, p. 167.

This gentleman, says Brother Long, is a wealthy local preacher in our Church, on Taylor's Island, Dorchester county, Md. Brothers McCarter and Lame confirm the statement.

In a letter dated Taylor's Island, Feb. 12, 1858, published in the *Cambridge* (Md.) *Eagle*, and signed "Levi D. Travers," we find the following. Speaking of Brother Long's exposure of his iniquity, he says:

"I now propose to speak in my own defence, before that court which my Ecclesiastical *Judge* has been pleased to arraign me. In his charge he has been very careful to state that I am a local preacher of the Methodist Episcopal Church—a truth I would not disguise. I am an humble local preacher of the said Church, a position I pray God I may never dishonor. I love the Methodist Episcopal Church; she is my spiritual mother. She took me in when I was a helpless infant; I have been rocked in her cradle, nurtured in her lap, educated in her school, and subscribe to her articles of religion and indorse her discipline, and desire no amendment. I prefer her to all the various branches of Christ's visible Church, because I believe her to be the truest resemblance of the Apostolic Church. I will battle upon her fields, fight under her banner while she holds to her Wesleyan discipline. But if she changes her colors I shall throw off all allegiance to her before her filibustering sons shall *spew* me out, and join myself to another division of the family of God. I am also charged with claiming property in the person of a negro man named Aaron Cornish, who ran away, and I offered a reward for his apprehension," &c.

Yes, this slaveholding Levite is a great Methodist! His phylactery is made very broad for his "spiritual mother," whose Discipline he dearly loves. But what of that rule, page 212, of this "Wesleyan Discipline:" "NO SLAVEHOLDER SHALL BE ELIGIBLE TO ANY OFFICIAL STATION IN OUR CHURCH HEREAFTER, &c.?" Does the Rev. Pharisee "endorse" that? Nay, but impiously tramples it under his feet. And all this time he dearly loves Methodism and the Discipline! Like a base parricide, who approaches his "mother" with well-affected blandishments and professions of filial regard, and then stabs her to the heart. And mark that threat, "if she changes her colors," &c. Such is the purpose of the Borderer generally—"If you alter the Discipline in the least, in regard to slavery, we will secede." "Look here, Mattison," said the late John A. Collins, of Baltimore, to us, at the last General Conference (calling us aside); "look here; what are you going to do at this General Conference?" "In respect to what, Brother Collins?" we calmly inquired. "Why, in regard to slavery," he answered. "Why," said we, "we intend to do all we can to put slavery out of the Methodist Episcopal Church." "Well," said he, "if you touch that subject we shall go by ourselves;"

and turned and walked off. And so from other Baltimore delegates; it was a common expression from the Border, "If you do as much as to dot an *i* or cross a *t* of the Discipline, in regard to slavery, we shall go by ourselves." And so Mr. Traverse: "If you do any thing to disturb my slaveholding, and slave-breeding, and slave-buying, I'll leave you!"

Brother Long says: "If the General Conference should ever make non-slaveholding and non-slavebreeding a test of membership, the Eastern Shore of Maryland will go to the Church South." Brother Lame says (page 23): "I have yet to find the man or Methodist with whom I have conversed, that has not expressed the same opinions precisely; and many contend that it should have gone with the great Southern secession." This is no doubt the general feeling on the Border; hence, as the best means of keeping them from seceding, Dr. BOND advised them, in case the General Conference of 1856 passed an extirpatory Rule, to preserve a "masterly inactivity"—that is, *nullify* the authority of the General Conference!

What a blessing it would be if all slaveholders *would* leave the Methodist Episcopal Church! the sooner the better. But if they do not leave or forsake their sins, God grant that the time may soon come when the Methodist Episcopal Church shall indeed "*spew them out of her mouth!*" They are like putrid carrion and rottenness in the temple of God.

But we have not yet done with this reverend slaveholder's confessions. Further on in his letter he says:

> "I am a slaveholder. I hold twenty slaves (right or wrong) under the sanction of the Constitution of the United States and the laws of Maryland. I hold them nearly all by inheritance; one half as the inheritance of my wife; of the other half, a portion I inherited from my father and son, a part were born of my slaves, and a part purchased. * * * * These slaves I have in my own family, and upon my lands, some of them acting as overseers. Now as a slaveholder I cannot conceive that as such I am rebelling against the righteous government of God."

Now don't be alarmed, my Methodist reader: "Brother Traverse" does not own but "twenty;" and of these he only "purchased" "part" of them. And besides, he is a good Methodist Local Preacher, within the bounds of the Philadelphia Conference, and "cannot conceive" that slaveholding is wrong! Moreover, he loves the Discipline dearly. The General Rule against slavery forbids the BUYING [mark] *or selling of men, women, or children, with an intention to enslave them.*

(p. 27); and "Brother Traverse" has "purchased" "part" of his "gang" of "twenty" to work on his "lands;" but then he loves the Discipline, and "desires no amendment!"

Brother Lame's pamphlet furnishes the following additional specimen of a slaveholding Local Preacher:

"During 1857, a member of the Methodist Episcopal Church, whose laudatory obituary appeared in the 'great official,' having died intestate, a black man belonging to the estate of the deceased, a Methodist also, was put on the block by the executors, and purchased by a colored local preacher on the same circuit. A short period after his purchase, the same piece of property decamped, as rumor says, owing to harsh treatment. He was apprehended, returned, taken to Baltimore, and offered to the Southern market, but his sale was spoiled by the constant assertion of the negro that his family connections, together with himself, was subject to fits; information that was perfectly correct. As far as we could learn, commiseration seemed to be felt for the local preacher." (p. 26.)

Now put all these facts together:—that we have *near a thousand* Local Preachers in slave territory—the statements of Dr. Lee and Dr. McFerrin—the admission of the Westmoreland memorial—the statement of Mr. Clemm—the case of Mr. Hutt—that of Mr. Traverse—and the one last above mentioned; and judge ye, whether, in all human probability, we have not this day at least FIVE HUNDRED LOCAL PREACHERS IN THE METHODIST EPISCOPAL CHURCH WHO ARE SLAVEHOLDERS!"*

That most of the 812 hold slaves, there can be no reasonable doubt; and that doing thus, they all trample upon the Discipline of the Church and the authority of God, is equally certain. And we have no question that men of this stamp are being ordained as deacons and elders in the slaveholding Conferences every year, as Mr. Clemm intimated at the Philadelphia Conference at Easton. But more of this hereafter.

---

* At the Annual Meeting of the Local Preachers' Association of New York and Brooklyn, October 3, 1858, there were, among those who spoke, six from slave territory; viz. HANNAN, COOK, ROBERTS, and BRADY, from Baltimore; and MCCULLUCH and RIDDLE, from Delaware. There were doubtless others who did not speak. Wonder how many slaveholders there were among them?

CHAPTER VI.

SLAVE-BUYING AND SLAVE-SELLING.

We have thus shown, in the last three chapters, that thousands of private members, class-leaders, stewards, trustees, and local preachers in our Church are slaveholders. But leaving the matter of mere slave*holding*, we propose now to show that *our members on the Border* BUY AND SELL SLAVES *with impunity*, precisely as do members of other Churches there, or "men of the world." The Discipline, as we have seen, expressly forbids "the buying or selling of men, women, or children, with the intention to enslave them." We have seen, also, how some of our local preachers respect these rules. Let us now inquire how far our private members on the Border (who, as our bishops inform us, "in respect to intelligence, piety, and attachment to Methodist discipline and economy, will compare favorably with other portions of the Church")* regard these rules.

I. Nearly all the increase of the slave population of Maryland and Virginia is sold to go to the more southern States. Slaves are their great staple export, and their chief source of revenue. By a report of a special committee of the House of Representatives of South Carolina, on slavery and the slave-trade, made in 1857, it appears that from 1840 to 1850, the increase of slaves in Maryland and Virginia was 30 per cent. Of these, the proportions exported to other States, and the number kept at home, are as follows:

Maryland exported......	26,270	Virginia exported......	111,259
Kept at home...........	631	Kept at home..........	23,441

Here we have 137,529 sold into life-long bondage on the sugar and cotton and rice fields of the far South, against 24,072 who remain in slavery at home; nearly six sevenths of the whole sold to go South!

Now when we remember that the chief wealth of these slave-breeding States consists of their slaves; and that the Methodists are the most numerous and influential and wealthy denomination in these States, it follows irresistibly that the Meth-

* Episcopal Address for 1856.—Journals, p. 200.

odists must be, even more than others, engaged in the breeding and selling of slaves for the Southern market.

II. In regard to the domestic slave-trade, Br. Long says:

"Since the publication of the first edition of my book, a friend inquired of me whether I had ever known one member of the Church to be arrested for selling a slave to another member of the Church. I answered that I never had. If one member of the Church wants money, and another member of the Church residing in the neighborhood wants a slave, the sale is made, and no more attention is paid to the sale than would be paid to the selling of a horse. It is not considered a violation of the Discipline, for it is but an exchange from one mercenary slaveholder to another. I know a recent case in which a member of the highest standing in the Church sold slaves to another member of equal standing; and the sale was regarded as a common business transaction. If a church-member who is a farmer needs a hand, he buys a slave, if he wishes to do so, either of saint or sinner, or at a public sale, as best suits his purpose, with the intention of reaping the fruits of his involuntary labor. I appeal to the preachers of the Philadelphia Conference if it is not so."—(Pages 400, 401.)

In close connection with the above, the same writer gives the following account of the kidnapping of the adopted child of a free colored man by a rich Methodist:

"A free colored man, and cousin of Frederick Douglass, who was liberated by Capt. Thomas Auld, of Talbot county (and I will just here say, without the knowledge or consent of Capt. Auld, that he has manumitted some six or eight young colored men and women since 1844), married a woman who was also free. They had no children of their own; but a free colored woman, on her decease, had left them her little daughter to bring up. This man was sober and industrious, and a good painter. The little girl was old enough to be of great service to his wife, who was afflicted with partial blindness. According to the laws of Maryland, a white man can seize a free colored man's children, take them before a magistrate, and have them bound to service against the consent of the parents. On the holy Sabbath, a rich Methodist, accompanied by a constable, went to the house of the colored delinquent brought before the Church. A committee was appointed; but the man was acquitted. And this moral and religious kidnapper is still in the Church, and, I suppose, contributes his mite towards sending missionaries to convert the heathen."—(Pages 401, 402.)

And yet, with such facts as these within their reach, there are men at the North, and even some Methodist preachers, who labor to quiet the people by affirming, that the *Methodist* slaveholding on the Border is of a very mild type—that there is but little of it, any way; and, as our bishops told us in their last Episcopal Address, that "the white membership there, in regard to intelligence, PIETY, and ATTACHMENT TO THE METHODIST DISCIPLINE AND ECONOMY, will compare favorably with other portions of the Church!!"

III. Upon the subject of buying and selling slaves, Brother McCarter writes as follows:

"Of these church-members there are those who purchase and sell slaves as they do any other property—who buy them that they may avail themselves of their unpaid toil, and who sell them as embarrassment, good prices, or vices in the slave may be provocatives to their transfer to others or to the South."—(Page 22.)

"Now no one who knows the Peninsula* will deny the statement, that the buying of men, women, and children, without any intention to free them, is a very usual, indeed, almost universal practice among Methodists who buy at all. If the *buying* of men, women, and children, with an intention to enslave them be any wrong, then we should like it shown that, since 1820, in our Conference, any one was ever before a committee therefor. It used to be that whenever a Methodist bought a slave, he knew that the Church required, and demanded his liberty; that if he declined to abide by the judgment of the Church, or refused, or neglected to bring the bought slave before the Church, that she might break the fetters from his limbs, the buyer would himself be disowned as a member of the Methodist Episcopal Church. But that day has long since passed, and the Methodist now stocks his farm with slaves as he would with grazing cattle; and it is no offence, and the Church never looks after the matter."—(*Border Methodism*, p. 62.)

In another part of his pamphlet, Brother McCarter has the following eloquent and pathetic passage:

"Not a road over which the members of the Philadelphia Annual Conference have passed, in Maryland and Virginia, but has been travelled by the manacled slave torn from the endearments of birthplace and kindred. Scarcely an altar of any church in which he has ministered, from which the slave has not been taken to return no more to that place in the church's gallery, where he was wont to worship and sing of heaven as the place where 'the slave should be free from his master.' And in many instances the Church's own dark children have been the victims of these cruel exportations.

"They have gone! but not by the tide of voluntary emigration, or by death, from our Churches. Their names have been lost to the class record, but they bore not with them a certificate of membership in the Methodist Episcopal Church to their distant bondage. Why should they? It would but enhance their market value, and put the more dollars into the pockets of the mercenary wretches, who would sell the religion of the slave by making the evidence of its possession the reason for a higher bid as he stood on the auction block. * * * *

"Each year in the slave population of Maryland and Virginia a large portion of the 'increase' is carried away into the more southern States. During the eleven years of Conference silence, how many thousands have been borne away in chains from the fields of labor occupied by the ministers of the Philadelphia Conference! Methodists, too, have helped to swell the number of those thus sold, and yet the Conference has been silent. Ah! in the Church's own bosom is the foul plague spot and her relation to

---

* "The Peninsula" is that part of the Philadelphia Conference lying in slave territory. It consists of the tongue of land lying between Chesapeake Bay and the seacoast, including Delaware, a part of Maryland, and two counties of Virginia.

slavery, in the connection of preachers, stewards, leaders, and private members with slaveholding—in this there is found the secret of silence to the enormities of the traffic in the world without; because the principle of *property in human beings* is conceded practically in the Church, and she can but be a very 'Satan reproving sin' by condemning the laws and usages which control movable property in its being carried to the highest market." —(Pages 13, 14.)

IV. While at the Philadelphia Conference at Easton, in March, 1858, we were told by one of its members (and he was not an "abolitionist" either), that he saw a colored boy whom he knew, go on board of a steamboat at Norfolk, bound for the South; and who had been sold to a slave-trader for the Southern market by his Methodist owner. He said the poor fellow looked wistfully towards the shore of his native land, as the boat moved off from the dock, and "wept as though his heart would break." He called him a "boy;" but in plantation parlance all male slaves are "boys," even if eighty years old. If a "boy" literally, the poor fellow might well weep that he was to see father and mother, brothers and sisters, no more in this world. It was a "long adieu" to them all, as the poor slave was borne away, to toil and die amid the rice or cotton fields of the far South. If a husband and father, as he might have been, he wept that he should see his wife and children no more. Has God, indeed, "an attribute that can take sides with such iniquity!" And yet there can be no question that Methodists in our Border Conferences are selling thousands every year, even for the Southern market.

V. We have before us a manuscript letter from a travelling preacher in the West, in which this sentence occurs:

"Four fugitive slaves from Missouri, passed through here yesterday, and shortly after four bloodhounds were on their track. * * * * I had a conversation with a slaveholder from Missouri, who told me that Methodists in that State bought, sold, bred, and hired slaves, the same as other people."

The writer of this letter is eminently responsible, and well known throughout the Methodist Episcopal Church.

VI. The following extract from Brother Long's "Pictures," will give the reader some idea *how* the sale of slaves is effected in modern times by Methodist producers:

"But it is contended that the members of the Church South can sell negroes to the traders in flesh and blood, when they please, but that our members can be expelled for such traffic. We will grant that this is the theory; but in practice there is very little difference, as far as my knowledge goes. There are many ways to avoid this rule and expulsion. Take an example.

"Brother Hardshell wants money; perhaps he has an extravagant family. He has made up his mind to sell a negro man; and as he must have an excuse, he charges him with impudence. His conscience goads him; and he is ashamed to tie him, and ride with him to the county town, and be caught bargaining with the negro-buyer. So he goes to Mr. Skinflint, who represents a class of men in the South that, for fifty cents, will give a woman stripped to her waist thirty-nine lashes, and offers him 25 dollars if he will come at night and take him to the negro-buyer: and this is done, according to contract. Perhaps weeks elapse before the preacher hears it, and then it is 'nigger news.' It is considered beneath the dignity of a gentleman to be prowling around negro-quarters to see if any slaves are missing. But should the preacher in charge call on Brother Hardshell, he demands *proof* that he ever sold a slave. There is no proof at hand. If he admits it, he charges the negro with being a thief, or being saucy, or with some other fault. This is about the end of the affair. And the preacher must not show too much zeal in the matter. If he does, the cry of 'abolitionist' will ring about his ears. Mr. Skinflint can procure among his associates plenty of tar and feathers."—(*Pictures*, pp. 53, 54.)

VII. That our members on the Border are induced to part with their surplus negroes, as others do, when they bring such enormous prices, and the slave-dealers come among them for "gangs," is rendered still more certain from the advertisements found in the county papers of that region. Take the following as indicating the amount of "trade" in that line, in the southern portion of the Philadelphia Conference. They are taken from a single number of the *Cambridge* (Md.) *Democrat*, January 20, 1858.

We are at all times purchasing SLAVES, paying the highest cash prices. Persons wishing to sell will call at No. 11 CAMDEN ST., Baltimore. Negroes received to BOARD. Communications addressed to WILSON & HINDES.

☞Any communications left with WM. H. GRACE, Esq., in Cambridge, will be attended to.

[Jan. 20, 1858 1y.

NEGROES WANTED.

I am again in the market, and will pay liberal prices in CASH for likely NEGROES who are slaves for life.

Persons having such property for sale, will do well to see me before they sell, as I will be at all times prepared to purchase. Communications addressed to me at Easton, or information left with SAMUEL R. VINTON, in Cambridge, will be promptly attended to.

WM. HARKER.

Jan. 20, 1858–3m*

VALUABLE NEGROES AT PUBLIC SALE.

By virtue of an order of the Orphans' Court of Dorchester County, I will, as acting Administrator of F. B. C. Turpin, expose at public sale, at the store of Henry Lord, at CROTCHER'S FERRY,

ON SATURDAY, FEB. 13th, 1858,

the following NEGROES, slaves for life: Negro woman MARIA, aged 65 years; negro woman MILLY, aged 20 years, and infant child about 2 months old.

The above negroes will be sold, in or out of the State, on a credit of six months, to the highest bidder. LOWDER SIRMAN,

Jan. 20, 1858–3t Acting Administrator.

POSTPONED SALE.

I will sell at PUBLIC SALE at the Court House door, in Cambridge

ON MONDAY NEXT, 25th inst.,

negro girl GEORGIANA, aged 16 years, slave for life.

Terms cash, or note with good security, payable in six months.

Jan. 20, 1858. W. R. PATTISON.

We see by the above how fast Methodism is doing away with slavery on the Border, by its compromising and let-alone policy; in a word, that it is spreading and fattening under the silence of Methodist ministers, and Methodist Annual and General Conferences. But there is a still darker shade to this terrible picture.

CHAPTER VII.

SLAVEHOLDING TRAVELLING PREACHERS.

From slaveholding and buying and selling among our private members, class-leaders, stewards, trustees, and local preachers, we proceed to show that we have now some six or eight open and avowed slaveholders, at least, among the members of our Border Conference. But our limits, which we are likely to overrun, will compel us to brevity.

I. In 1855, Dr. J. Cross, now of the Methodist Episcopal Church South, informed us personally, that *he knew* of some members of the Baltimore Conference, who owned slaves, though they were held in the name of others.

II. In the winter of 1856, Dr. M. F. Deems, also a preacher in the Southern Church, and a slaveholder, informed us that *he knew* several of the members of our Border Conferences to be slaveholders.

III. In December, 1856, Dr. McFerrin, editor of the *Nashville Christian Advocate*, addressed several letters to Bishop Morris through the columns of his paper. In the first of these letters he makes the following declarations:

"You have this day many large slaveholders in your division of the Church. You know that in Maryland and Virginia you have hundreds, yea, thousands of members who hold slaves; that you have ordained deacons and elders in the ministry of your Church who are slaveholders. You yourself have ordained to the office and work of the ministry many a slaveholder. Why, then, in the name of our common Christianity, should the Southern Church be persecuted and denounced because she does what your own branch of the Church constantly practises? Let us see. The Methodist Episcopal Church South has in her communion slaveholders. So has the Methodist Episcopal Church North. The Methodist Episcopal Church South has in the ministry ordained deacons and elders who are slaveholders. So has the Methodist Episcopal Church North. These slaveholders in the South were elected to the work and office of the ministry by the Annual Conferences of the South. So were those elected by the Conferences belonging to the Northern division. They were ordained by the laying on of the hands of the bishops. Bishop Waugh, Bishop Morris, and Bishop Janes, to my certain knowledge, have each ordained slaveholders to the office of deacon and elder. Where, then, is the difference? perhaps the principal difference, and the only one worth mentioning, is that the South, occupying a much larger slave territory than the North, has a greater number of ministers and members connected with slavery than are found in the North! Yet the principle is the same. And your late General Conference refused to make non-slaveholding a test of membership. True, a majority was in favor of inserting a rule to that effect, but not a constitutional majority; so that your Discipline tolerates slaveholders in the ministry and membership. Where, then, in view of these facts, is there cause for a war upon the Southern Church, especially as waged by those who call themselves conservative men?"

If the facts here alleged are true (and we have every reason to believe they are), there is much cogency in Dr. McFerrin's reasoning. "Thou that sayest a man should not steal, dost thou steal?" We are hardly prepared to cast the mote out of the eye of the Methodist Episcopal Church South, blind as she is, till we get the beam out of the eye of the Methodist Episcopal Church North. For slavery to cast out slavery, is too much like casting out devils through Beelzebub the prince of devils. Indeed, in one respect the Southern Church have the advantage of us—they *profess nothing better* than pro-slavery, and justify themselves by the Bible; while we condemn slaveholding; profess "anti-slavery;" and yet have thousands of slaveholders in the Church. In other words, we are an "anti-slavery" slaveholding Church!

As to the statement of Dr. McFerrin, that four of our bishops have each ordained men to the office of deacon and elder in the Church, we understand him to speak of such ordination *since the separation* in 1845; as Dr. JANES was not a bishop prior to that time. Whether these ordinations were of local or travelling preachers, Dr. M. does not specify. Neither does he indicate whether or not these bishops were aware, at the time, that they were ordaining slaveholders.

The most charitable construction, therefore, is, that they were local preachers in the slaveholding Conferences; and that the bishops ordaining them were not aware that they were slaveholders. So far, then, the extract bears mainly upon points discussed in preceding chapters—the number of slaveholding laymen, local deacons, and elders.

But the first paragraph bears upon slaveholding in the travelling ministry. If "slaveholders have been in the General Conference from the first delegated General Conference TILL THIS DAY," they must have been in those of 1848, '52, and '56; all since the division. These slaveholding delegates are probably the men who have assured us, from time to time, that there was very little slaveholding on the border. But Dr. McFerrin explains himself more fully in a subsequent paper.

Rev. F. G. HIBBARD, on seeing Dr. McFerrin's statements, denied their correctness, whereupon Dr. M. reaffirms them as follows:

"What are we to understand by these remarks? Does Dr. Hibbard disbelieve our statements, when we affirm that preachers and ordained ministers in connection with his Church are slaveholders? We did not say that any travelling preachers are *ostensibly* slaveholders. We are aware that in the Baltimore Conference, but few if any of the travelling preachers hold the right of slave property in their own name. But how many are connected with families holding slaves? We cannot tell how many; but we do know, personally, some who are in this category. And we could give the names of some in high places, whose children, if not themselves and wives, are interested in slaves as property.

"Does he disbelieve us, when we state that local preachers and ordained ministers in the local ranks in the Methodist Episcopal Church North are slaveholders? Does he disbelieve us, when we affirm that members of his Church, in Maryland and Virginia, by hundreds, are slaveholders; owning slaves as property; inheriting slaves; buying slaves; selling slaves, as their wishes or convenience may dictate? If he will not credit our statements, we ask him to go to Baltimore; to the planting counties of Maryland; to many counties in Virginia, and investigate for himself; and if he do not, after a faithful examination, find our words true, then will we make the *amende honorable* through the columns of this paper. We refer him to Rev. Thos. O. Summers, D.D., Book Editor, in the Publishing House, at

Nashville, Tenn., who was formerly a member of the Baltimore Conference, and filled stations in the city of Baltimore, and labored extensively in Maryland and Virginia, and if he will not state that members in the Methodist Episcopal Church in all these places are slaveholders, and many of them extensive slaveholders, and that class-leaders, stewards, and preachers are slaveholders, then we will retract what we have said.

"Dr. Hibbard has been imposed upon, and has been made to believe that there is no indiscriminate slaveholding among the members of his Church in Maryland and Virginia. What does he mean by *indiscriminate* slaveholding? Is to inherit slaves, to buy slaves, to sell slaves without any reference to their emancipation, but as property, indiscriminate slaveholding? Then are ministers and members of the Methodist Episcopal Church North slaveholders, in the same sense that other citizens of the slaveholding States are slaveholders.

"We admit that a *majority* of the preachers in the Northern connection are opposed to slavery; we admit that many of them, with thousands of the laity, are aiming to extirpate slaveholding, both in the local ministry and in the membership; yet this admission does not change the facts in the case, and we think Dr. H., or any of his brethren, should not repudiate the Southern Church, or quarrel with their brethren in the South, while in his own Church there are hundreds, it not thousands, of bona-fide slaveholders, and no rule in the Discipline for their expulsion. They are, to use Dr. Stevens' language, 'constitutionally, historically, and administratively' a slaveholding Church."

In the preceding extract we have the following important points:

1. That travelling preachers in the Baltimore Conference are slaveholders; and that Dr. McFerrin intended to include such in his first statements.

2. That the children of some "in high places," if not themselves and wives, are interested in slave property. Who are meant by "some in high places," we cannot positively say, but we suppose he must mean some of our bishops. We have understood that the children of Bishop WAUGH had slaves in their families; but whether owned or hired, we never learned. Bishop MORRIS has a son who is a preacher in the Methodist Episcopal Church South; but whether he is a slaveholder or not we cannot say. Bishop AMES had a daughter married in Indianapolis, by Bishop WAUGH, during the session of the last General Conference, to a gentleman living in Baltimore; but whether he is a slaveholder or not we are not informed. We suppose, however, from Dr. McFerrin's remarks, that he alludes to some one of these cases; and that he intends to convey the idea that one or more of these children of our bishops are "interested in slaves as property." It is said of the sons of Eli, that their sin was great before the Lord, "for men abhorred the offering of the Lord." And God expostulated with

him, saying, "Wherefore kick ye at my sacrifice and at mine offering, which I have commanded in mine habitation; and *honorest thy sons above me*, to make yourselves fat with the chiefest of all the offerings of Israel my people?"* His wrong as a father and priest was, that he did not by authority restrain his sons from a course of conduct that brought disgrace upon the house of God. And so in these cases: if blame attaches to either of our bishops, it is for ever consenting that their children should become connected with slavery, either directly by marriage, or otherwise.

3. The expression, "if not themselves," is a very broad hint, to say the least, that some one of our bishops themselves may be indirectly connected with slavery, as Bishop Andrew was in 1844. For his slaves were the "property" of his wife, and became his only by marriage.

4. Dr. M. is very explicit as to slave-buying and selling among our members on the border—"*buying* slaves, *selling* slaves, as their wishes or convenience may dictate."

5. Dr. Stevens is quoted as fully sustaining Dr. M., that we are "constitutionally, historically, and administratively a slave-holding Church." And what better fulcrum could any man wish upon which to rest his lever to overturn all our pretensions to "anti-slavery," than this scandalous allegation of Dr. Stevens, the foulest slander ever yet uttered against the Methodist Episcopal Church? But taken as a whole, Dr. McFerrin not only corroborates the testimony adduced in the preceding chapters, as to slaveholding among private members, official members, local deacons and elders, but also implicates, as involved in slaveholding, travelling ministers, if not some of our bishops themselves! Whether this last intimation be well founded or not, the connection of the families of some of our bishops may serve to explain the fact of their very strong conservatism in regard to slavery.

IV. Alluding to the denial of Brother Hibbard, Dr. LEE, of the *Richmond Christian Advocate*, confirms the statements of Dr. McFerrin in the following emphatic manner:

"Sir, is it not known to *you*, and to *me*, and to *many*, *many others*, that in the church in which Bishop Simpson and Dr. McClintock are ministers, and from which they were delegates to the Wesleyan Methodist Church, there are thousands and thousands of slaves, and that these slaves are

* 1 Samuel, ii. 17, 29.

owned and worked from sun to sun by the *members* and *ministers* of said church? Will Bishop Simpson, or Dr. McClintock, or the New York Express, or any one else, undertake to deny that there are many slaveholders and slaveworkers among the *private* members, and *official* members, and *ministers* of the Northern division of the Methodist Episcopal Church? They will not try it. It cannot be denied."

And again:

"If you never knew it before, learn it now from me—*the preachers and people in the Northern division of the Methodist Episcopal Church hold slaves as truly as those in the Southern division.* Now, try and remember this in future."

This extract is also in point; not only corroborating what we have before proved, that private members and official members on the Border hold slaves by "thousands and thousands," but that "ministers" and "preachers," also, are deeply involved in this iniquity.

V. Rev. THOMAS CARLTON, Book Agent, informed us at the Book Room, in New York, in the winter of 1855, that Rev. S. G. ROSZEL, of the Baltimore Conference, was the owner of three slaves. This he admitted subsequently at the session of the Black River Conference, held in Potsdam, N. Y., June, 1857, in the presence of some twenty witnesses; and also at the session of the East Genesee Conference, held at Canandaigua, N. Y., in August, 1857, before some forty of the preachers. He also admitted at this last place, and at the same time, that he had known of another member of the same Conference who owned twelve slaves, who undertook to settle them in Pennsylvania, but they all went back to him. Whether these slaves are still owned by a Methodist preacher, or have been shifted into other hands, or sold to go further South, Brother C. did not inform us. But from all the light we can get upon the subject, we have reason to believe that Mr. Roszel, at least, is still a slaveholder in the Baltimore Conference.

VI. We know from the most positive evidence that there have been for years, and are still, several slaveholders among the members of the Philadelphia Conference.

"A widow of one of the preachers of the Philadelphia Annual Conference," says Brother Long, "died since January of the present year [1858]. She resided in Maryland; she was wealthy, and a slaveholder. Shortly before her decease she gave three or four hundred dollars towards building for our preachers one of the finest parsonages on the Eastern Shore of Maryland. She left a portion of her wealth to the Methodist Episcopal Church South."*

VII. Rev. John Bayne, a member of the Conference, died at Cochranville, Chester county, Pa., Aug. 6, 1852.† After his death a will was found in his handwriting, duly signed, but not witnessed, and supposed to have been written during his last sickness. By that will it appeared that he was the owner of seven slaves in Maryland, and that he designed to free them at his death. But as the will was not *witnessed*, it was not a legal instrument.

It so happened, however, that some years previously, Mr. Bayne had licensed Rev. Andrew Manship, now Tract Agent of the Philadelphia Conference, as an exhorter; and Mr. Manship still had the license, with Mr. Bayne's signature attached; and, as by the provisions of the will, it was evident that Mr. Bayne intended that his slaves should be free at his death, his administrator, Rev. I. F. Boone, M. D., of the Philadelphia Conference, applied to the Court of Cecil county, Md., for the freedom of the slaves. Mr. Manship and another witness appeared before the court, and made oath to the handwriting of Mr. Bayne, and upon their testimony the will was declared valid, and the seven slaves were set at liberty. We had all these principal facts from Mr. Manship himself, who stated them openly, at the seat of the Conference, March 29th, 1858, in presence of Rev. Mr. McCarter and Rev. Henry Sutton, both members of the same Conference. Mr. Manship bore the joyful tidings of liberty to at least one of the slaves, and described the glowing rapture of her heart when she first learned that she was FREE.

VIII. Rev. Wm. Quinn, a member of the Conference, is the owner of some twenty slaves. In 1852 (the year that all the members of the Conference were asked, "*Are you a slaveholder?*") he was known to be a slaveholder, and a resolution was adopted by the Conference, requiring him to manumit his slaves. To keep up a show of obedience, he had deeds of manumission recorded, to take effect when each slave is thirty-five years old. Even the children of these manumitted slaves,

---

* Pictures of Slavery, p. 385. † Minutes for that year, p. 20.

and their children after them, are held by this model Methodist preacher till thirty-five years old; and then, when hard toil has stiffened their limbs, and begun to bleach their locks—when their children have grown up around them, still in slavery, and the winter of life is coming on apace—*then*, if they are willing to sever the ties that for thirty years have been binding them to the old plantation, and start out for themselves when the best of life is gone, then they may be free! The juice of the orange has been pressed out for the use of the clerical master, and the poor old worn-out negroes may now take the worthless rind, if they wish. This is Mr. Quinn's own showing.* He even claims it as a virtue that his slaves are all manumitted, to be free at thirty-five! A friend of his, in apologizing for him, said that by freeing them at that age he had lost several thousand dollars!

This same Methodist preacher admitted that he had sent a slave to Baltimore, and sold him, but alleged as an excuse that the slave was a thief, and was liable to be arrested and convicted, in which case he would be sold to go South. It was simply the old excuse of all Methodist slave-sellers—"He was a bad nigger, and I had to sell him"—though put into a little more pious form. Like all Mr. Quinn's slaves, "the boy" was "manumitted," to be free at thirty-five; and Mr. Quinn claimed that it was a benevolent act to sell him in Baltimore till thirty-five, and prevent his being sold to go South for life. But for the alleged theft, we have only the word of the slave-seller, who had every motive for fabricating the charge. He must, of course, justify his crime against God and his fellow-man, and how natural that he should frame the old apology, that the slave was a thief, especially as every slave who eats an onion, or a chicken, raised by over-work, and on his own little "patch," if allowed one, is nevertheless a "thief" in the eye of slavery.

But mark how Dr. Stevens fixed up this case, in the *New York Advocate*. He says:

> "A statement was read from a letter to the Conference, wherein Mr. Quinn affirmed that he had disposed of a boy in the city of Baltimore, who, as a felon, was about to be sent South."

---

* The reader should understand that the writer attended the last session of the Philadelphia Conference (March, 1858) as counsel for Rev. J. D. Long. We write therefore, upon these cases, from what we *saw* and *heard* personally, and not from mere rumor or hearsay.

Now we heard the letter from Mr. Quinn read, and the remarks made upon it; and we positively affirm that this is a gross misrepresentation, if not a slander upon the poor dumb negro. Even Mr. Quinn did not allege any thing of the kind. The idea conveyed by Mr. Stevens is, that the negro had been *arrested*, and *convicted as a felon*, and as such was "about to be sent South;" not a word of which is true.

The whole case is this: a Methodist preacher of the Philadelphia Conference sent a slave to market and sold him, and when called to an account for it, offered as an excuse that "the boy" had stolen, and was *liable* to be taken up, and sold to go South. For the truth of this showing, we appeal to Drs. COOPER, and DURBIN, and HODGSON, and even to Dr. QUIGLEY himself, who defended Mr. Quinn. The apology manufactured for him by Dr. Stevens, is wholly gratuitous, and without foundation. He has volunteered to screen a slaveholding and slave-selling Methodist preacher, and in so doing has libelled a poor dumb slave. May the Lord pity all such editors! But what did the Conference do in relation to this case? They first passed the following:

"*Resolved*, That the character of the Rev. Mr. Quinn be passed, and that the inquiry into what he has done in reference to manumitting his slaves, in pursuance to his promises to the Conference at its session of 1842, be referred to a commission to be hereafter appointed to ascertain the facts and particulars in the case, and report the same to the Conference at its next session."

This Mr. Stevens was very careful to quote. But was the "commission" ever appointed? Never. Instead of announcing their names at the opening of the next session, as is customary in such cases, the matter was allowed to hang, day after day, till near the close of the session, when the preceding resolution was reconsidered, and the whole subject *laid on the table!* This Dr. Stevens did not publish, but left his readers to suppose that a commission was actually put upon the track of the slaveholding preacher.

Here, then, we have a member of the Philadelphia Conference, who has been a slaveholder since 1842, or for *sixteen years past*, at least; and *known* to be such by every member of the Conference. He has now twenty or more slaves, and is raising more as fast as he can, and has even commenced selling off his superabundant stock. And yet, what of it? What did the Conference do with him?—simply, *nothing!*

The proposed commission was a sham from the beginning. The Conference had all the facts before them, and knew, without appointing a commission, that Mr. Quinn was an open transgressor of the law of the Church, and of their own Conference rule in relation to his case, passed sixteen years ago.

By passing his case as they did, the Conference most emphatically *sanctioned slaveholding*, and slave-*breeding* and *selling*, by members of the Conference. Mr. Quinn is thus ecclesiastically whitewashed, and slavery and the slave-trade sanctified. As Mr. Quinn's character passed, the following resolution was offered:

"*Resolved*, That it is the sense of this Conference, that its requisition upon its members [mark!] to manumit their slaves, according to the Discipline, shall be twenty-one years or under. J. CUNNINGHAM, C. J. THOMPSON."

But this resolution was tabled in an instant, with clapping of hands; and though two efforts were subsequently made by Brother Cunningham to get it up and act upon it, in one instance another subject was called up at once, and in the other no attention was paid to the motion. So the case was left.*

IX. Rev. E. J. WAY, on his name being called, arose and said: "I am a native of Pennsylvania. I have married two wives on the Peninsula [Md.], both of whom were the daughters of slaveholders. On the death of my first father-in-law, he left ten slaves, of whom a part fell to me. They were all manumitted [that is, to be free, as we learned, at a future period, say at thirty-five years of age]. Some of the slaves had been sold, for one of whom $650 was realized. Of this amount, $60 fell to me, though I have not yet received it. I have proposed to my wife to invest it for the benefit of Jim, when his time is out, that he may go to Liberia, or take it and go East with it, and invest it in abolition tracts, or any thing else he chooses." [Great laughter.] We read the above to Mr. Way

* In the management of this and other cases at the same Conference, there were, in our view, strong grounds of complaint against the presiding bishop, both as respects his administration, and the manner in which he seemed to regard the slaveholders on the one hand, and the anti-slavery men of the Conference on the other. But as those matters will be reviewed hereafter in a more "official" manner, we shall dispose of them in this pamphlet by a merely passing notice in another chapter. If any reader would like to read the proceedings of that memorable Conference in detail, let him inclose 24 cents in stamps to the writer, No. 16 West Forty-first street, New York, and we will send him "*Border Methodism and Border Slavery*," by J. M. McCarter, a member of the Conference, who was present, and, like ourself, took full notes of all the proceedings.

at the time, and he admitted its entire correctness. His character was passed without a question.

Rev. M. D. KURTZ's name being called, Brother Long arose and said he had good reason for believing that he was connected with slavery. His presiding elder thought his connection was justified. Mr. Kurtz said he had no connection with slavery, except an involuntary connection. There were two or three slaves in whom his wife had an interest, but they were all manumitted, to be free at twenty-eight and thirty. He denied that he had any *improper* connection with slavery.

Rev. Mr. BISHOP moved that the commission appointed to inquire into the case of Brother Quinn, be instructed to inquire into the circumstances of Brother Kurtz's slaveholding also. Dr. Durbin opposed the motion. At this point the chair arrested the discussion, pending Brother Bishop's motion, by calling the name of the next elder on the list, leaving, as we supposed, the case of Brother Kurtz as laid over. But, as subsequent events proved, his character was thus passed, *without a vote of Conference*, though arrested by Brother Long, and upon his own admission a slaveholder!

XI. Rev. J. R. MERRILL, when his name was called, wished all to hear what he was about to say. He had stated, some days before, that he could convince the most ultra abolitionist that his slaveholding was benevolent. About four years since a colored man came into his possession [did not say how]. He wrote to a friend to tell the boy [all colored men are "boys," if a hundred years old] to go to work for himself, and when he could come and manumit him, he would do so. ["Manumit," i. e., to be free at thirty-five or fifty, or at death.] When he went over where the boy was, he found a strong prejudice in the community against his manumission, on the ground that he was a drunkard. He did not know what to do, but told the boy to go to work, and as soon as he became *reliable* he would manumit him. He hired him out, and directed his agent to give him half his wages, keeping the other half for the future benefit of the slave. He was obliged to hold him, in self-defence. [Brother Long whispered to us—"This is a case of *sanctified* slaveholding."] If the boy had been manumitted he would have become a miserable fellow, and been pointed at as a specimen of "free niggers." He held him, therefore, as a slave, first, for the good of the slave, and secondly, that he might not, by freeing him, injure the cause of emancipation, which the abolitionists professed to love so well. But though he believed the position of the boy as a slave was the best for *him* and for the cause, he would do as the Conference said in regard to his emancipation.

Rev. WM. COOPER said he appreciated the benevolence of Brother Merrill, but the Discipline required the manumission of the slave, if held by a Methodist preacher; and if Brother Merrill did not let go of the slave, the Conference would have to let go of him.

Brother Long said the excuse of Brother Merrill for still holding the slave in bondage was, that he was *intemperate*, when the fact might be that the poor bondman had fled to the intoxicating bowl under the influence of *despair*, in view of his being held in slavery by a Methodist preacher!

This last remark produced quite a sensation in the Conference, whereupon the bishop rushed over the case by calling the name of the next elder on the list. "Nothing against Brother R.," was responded, when a brother arose and said—"I am not satisfied with the disposition of the case of Brother Merrill. I move, that it is the judgment of this Conference, that Brother Merrill should manumit his slave."

The motion was put, and prevailed.

To a person not acquainted with the Border method of interpreting the Discipline, this may look a little anti-slaverywise. But "be not deceived." "Should manumit his slave," simply meant to record a deed of manumission by which he should be free *at some future time*, say ten or twenty or thirty years hence. A similar resolution was passed in regard to Mr. Quinn in 1842, and the way he complied with it was to manumit his slaves to be free at thirty-five, and their children at the same age; and the Conference at its last session (1858) practically endorsed this kind of manumission, as meeting the requirements of the Discipline!

Conversing with a prominent member of the Conference upon the subject, he said that the laws of Maryland forbade emancipation after the slave was forty years of age; but as the Discipline only required the preacher to "execute, if it be practicable, a deed of manumission," &c., without specifying *when* the slave was to be made free by it, if the deed made him free at thirty-nine years, eleven months, and twenty-nine days of age, under the laws of the State, the preacher had met the requirement of the Discipline. So Mr. Quinn keeps his slaves till they are thirty-five—within five years of as long as he can and free them at all—and *then* lets them go if they wish to! And then even claims it as a most benevolent act, and "all for conscience' sake!"

Now we regard this as the most cruel and hypocritical of all slaveholding. Kept till the best of life is gone; tantalized with the hope of freedom which few live to enjoy; stimulated thus to extra exertion for his master; his children still retained in slavery; the enormities of common slaveholding are even augmented; and the accursed institution is perpetuated from generation to generation. And yet such is the accepted interpretation of the rule, and the practice of the preachers under it, in the Philadelphia Conference! Its obvious meaning is, that "whenever any travelling preacher becomes an owner of a slave or slaves, by any means," as by marriage or bequest, "he shall forfeit his ministerial character in our Church, unless he execute, if it be practicable, a *legal* EMANCIPATION,"* not a deed of manumission to take effect ten or twenty years hence. But they meet the rule by executing a "deed of manumission," to take effect, if the poor slave lives, years and years afterwards. Hence the stress laid upon their "deeds of manumission" in the case of Mr. Quinn and in the case following.

XII. Rev. WM. WARNER, of the same Conference, is also a slaveholder. When his name was called before the Conference, he arose and said he had inherited several slaves from his father's estate, whom he still owned; but they were all "manumitted," to be free, the females at twenty-five and the boys at twenty-eight, and their issue at the same age. He believed himself justified in his course, both by the Discipline and the Bible. The bishop called another name, and so Mr. Warner's character was passed.

Thus we have not only the testimony of Drs. CROSS and DEEMS and MCFERRIN and LEE to the general fact that we have slaveholders now in the travelling ministry, on the Border; but also a clear case of one slaveholder in the Baltimore Conference; of one widow of a travelling preacher who was

* "EMANCIPATE. To set free from bondage; to restore to liberty.
"EMANCIPATION. The act of setting free from slavery; deliverance from bondage."
—*Webster.*

a slaveholder; of one member of the Philadelphia Conference who died in 1852 the owner of seven slaves; and of five members of that body who are now slaveholders, owning from one to twenty! And in one case a venerable elder had even sold one of his slaves!! And all this is *allowed* by that body of two hundred Christian ministers, with one of our bishops at their head! Not the slightest whisper of disapprobation was heard in regard to any one of them. The great effort on all hands, with the exception of some half a dozen men, was, as God is witness of the truth, and we must answer to HIM in the Last Day, to *cover up the iniquity*, and SCREEN THE SLAVEHOLDING PREACHERS FROM BOTH EXPOSURE AND JUSTICE!! Yea, and while we pen these lines, the slaves of these ☞ Methodist Preachers! (Heaven pity us!) are toiling in bondage under the eye and lash of their overseers! O Lord! how long! how long!!

Of the number of slaves held by all these Methodists—private members, leaders, trustees and stewards, exhorters, local and travelling preachers—we cannot of course speak definitely. But all the known facts point to the unwelcome conclusion that they are to be numbered by tens of thousands. As confirmatory of the general estimates on pages 43, 44, take the following additional, and even more conclusive considerations. The census of 1850, taken in connection with our annual Minutes, shows that there cannot be less than ONE HUNDRED THOUSAND human beings now held in slavery by members of the Methodist Episcopal Church.

That the Methodists are numerous and wealthy, and hold slaves in great numbers, in Delaware, Maryland, and Virginia, will not be doubted. It is attested, on all hands, by those who know, and is not denied now, even by the veriest apologists for slavery. This being unquestionable, let us look at certain other facts and figures:

1. By the last census (1850), there were 3,204,313 slaves in the United States, with a regular increase of 100,000 a year. This will give us now (1858), over four millions of slaves. But take the census of 1850—3,204,313 slaves. Of these, 914,376 (which is 113,298 *more than one fourth of the whole*) are held within the present limits of the Methodist Episcopal Church! We have the very breeding-grounds of slavery for the whole South still left within our border. Indeed, what Ireland has for years been to Romanism in this country, Delaware, Mary-

land, and Virginia are to the more Southern States. Let not this most important fact (as shown on page 43) be lost sight of.

2. By De Bow's Compendium, page 95, we find that there are only 347,525 slaveholders, who own the 3,204,313 slaves; which gives an average of over nine slaves to each slaveholder in the United States. If, therefore, we have only 15,000 slaveholders in the Methodist Episcopal Church (which we believe to be a low estimate), and they hold an average number of slaves with other slaveholders, there must be 135,000 slaves now held in this republic by the professed followers of John Wesley! We mean, of course, in the M. E. Church proper.

3. The census, as shown on page 43 of this pamphlet, reports 136,958 slaveholders and 914,376 slaves as still within the present limits of the Methodist Episcopal Church. This will give an average of six and two thirds slaves to each slaveholder *in that particular territory*. If, therefore, our 15,000 Methodist slaveholders on the Border, who are known to be among the most wealthy citizens, hold as many slaves on an average as other slaveholders do in the same localities, we cannot have less than 100,000 slaves held by the 15,000 slaveholders.

This we believe to be the solemn and dreadful truth; that we have this day more than ONE HUNDRED THOUSAND SLAVES held by members of the Methodist Episcopal Church in the Border Conferences!

Now let us sum up the testimony adduced in the preceding chapters, in regard to the connection of the Methodist Episcopal Church with slavery. We have shown—

First, That our original position was one of theoretical and practical hostility to slavery, in all its moods and tenses—that JOHN WESLEY and his early followers were all abolitionists—that WATSON, and CLARKE, and BRADBURN, and GARRETTSON were abolitionists—that our first two bishops, COKE and ASBURY, were abolitionists—that MCKENDREE, our fourth bishop, was an abolitionist; and, indeed, that all the first Methodists, from 1739 to 1784, whether in England or America, were abolitionists. We have also proved, what no sane man who knows the facts will deny, that the Methodist Episcopal Church was organized in 1784 upon the most thorough abolition principles; and with a fixed and avowed determination on the part of our fathers, now with God, not only to extirpate slavery from the

Methodist Episcopal Church (for there were a few slaveholders then among the Methodists), but also from the republic.

Second, We have shown that from 1784 to 1844, the encroachments of slavery were gradual and incessant, till we were called upon to either take a stand against it, or tolerate it in the highest office in the Church, viz., in the Episcopacy. For half a century the legislation of the Church has been shaping itself more and more to the growing demands of slavery, and the increasing corruption of the Church by it, till in 1843 and 1844 we lost some 400,000 members by secession, all chargeable to slavery.

Third, That notwithstanding the great Southern secession, there was slave territory enough left in the Methodist Episcopal Church, and slaveholders enough, to corrupt us to the heart—that we have now from ten to twenty thousand slaveholders in our Church; among whom are hundreds of leaders, stewards, trustees, exhorters and local preachers, deacons, and elders, who own, raise, buy, and sell slaves, as suits their convenience and interest, and with utter impunity.

Fourth, That there cannot be less than ONE HUNDRED THOUSAND SLAVES now owned, and held in bondage by METHODISTS, in the *Northern portion* of the original Methodist Episcopal Church; and,

Finally, That we have from ten to twenty travelling preachers, more or less, in the Border Conferences, who openly hold slaves, from one to twenty each, without the slightest censure or disapproval on the part of the Conferences with which they stand connected; and that no efforts are made on the part of the executive authorities of the Church to stay this incoming tide of sin and corruption.

Now if any man can look these facts in the face, and not say that we are infinitely worse off, so far as connection with slavery is concerned, than we were before the division of 1844, we envy him not his knowledge, or judgment, or candor. Much as it may mortify our denominational pride, we may better own the whole truth, and by God's help seek to recover ourselves out of the snare of the devil, than to conceal, or refuse to look at the truth, till it is too late to retrieve our lost character and moral power. So far as this subject is concerned, the Methodist Episcopal Church in America is a fallen Church. She has sadly departed from her original position and character. To-day there are over 2000 travelling, and 5000 local Methodist preachers in the South; with a Discipline that even allows what the laws of Congress pronounce "piracy;" and preaching that slavery is of God, and perfectly consistent with all the requirements of the Bible. And in the Northern portion we are hastening on to the same consummation, so far as our slave territory is concerned, as fast as time and the Powers of Darkness can hurry us to ruin. Bating what genuine anti-slavery principle there is in the Northern Conferences, from the crown of the head to the soles of the feet there is no soundness in us, but wounds, and bruises, and putrefying sores; that have not been bound up, neither mollified with ointment. And our condition in this respect is growing worse and worse, every year, and every day.

Such is the present connection of the Methodist Episcopal Church with SLAVERY! Think of it, ye men of God who read these pages! Think of it, ye disgraced and outraged ministers of the Northern Conferences, our "companions in arms!" Think of it, ye Leaders and Stewards and Exhorters who breathe the free air of the North! Think of it, ye six thousand Local Preachers, Deacons, and Elders, who are laboring for God and Methodism in the Free States! Think of it! The Church of WESLEY, and BRADBURN, and FLETCHER, and COKE, and ASBURY, and GARRETTSON, and MCKENDREE—the Church of Class Meetings, and Love Feasts, and Camp Meetings, and Revivals—the Church of Free Grace, the Witness of the Spirit, and Entire Sanctification—a Church once torn asunder East and West by slavery, like the rending of an earthquake—*this* Church, and *such* a Church, in this land of liberty, and in 1859, with thousands of slaveholders in her bosom; hundreds in her local ministry; and from six to twenty, we know not how many, even among the travelling ministers!! Oh! "tell it not in Gath, publish it not in the streets of Askelon, lest the daughters of the Philistines rejoice, lest the daughters of the uncircumcised triumph."

Christian reader! Are you satisfied with such a state of things, even if it should grow no worse? Are you willing to have our beloved Church and our common Christianity thus corrupted and caricatured and scandalized by a few thousand slaveholders still left on our Southern Border; not more than one in twenty of our entire membership? Do *you* say, "Keep quiet—don't agitate the subject—don't bring these facts out before our people," &c.? God forbid! Christ from above cries out to you and us, "CRY ALOUD AND SPARE NOT!" The shining hosts of Methodists beyond the grave, respond: "Cry! CRY! CRY!! Lift up your voices like trumpets! Show the people their transgressions, and the house of Israel their sins." WESLEY, and COKE, and ASBURY, and MCKENDREE, and GEORGE, and EMORY, and HEDDING, and WAUGH—all *now* join in the celestial mandate, "Cry! *Cry!!* CRY!!! and save from utter corruption and ruin the CHURCH, which Christ has purchased with his own blood!"

Have we not, as a Church, slept over this subject long enough already? Have we not suffered enough and been disgraced enough by it? Is it not time that *something* was done, not only to arrest the onward march of slavery in our Church, but to either bring our thousands of slaveholders to repentance and reformation, or drive them from among us? If our beloved Bishops will not take down the scourge, and drive these money-changers from God's temple, should not the Northern ministry and laity do it? We think they should. And for the love we bear to Christ, to the world, and to the Methodist Episcopal Church—the Church of our spiritual birth and toil—we intend to do all we can with tongue and pen and money, as God may enable us, to bring about such a result in 1860. Precisely *what* should be done, we will endeavor briefly to sketch in the next chapter.

CHAPTER VIII.

WHAT SHOULD BE DONE FOR THE EXTIRPATION OF SLAVERY.

"*What shall be done for the extirpation of the evil of slavery?*" has been a standing inquiry in the Discipline for more than sixty years; and yet, what has been done? All this time slavery has been increasing in the Church, till in 1844 and 1845 it reached a crisis; first driving off some 20,000 members and 200 ministers in the North, and next taking with it 350,000 members and 2000 ministers in the South. But a seed of iniquity was left behind. The amputation was too low down. The gangrene left upon the bleeding stump has again infected the whole body. We are absolutely worse off to-day, so far as connection with slavery is concerned, than we were in 1844. Then we did not know of half the slaveholding in the membership, in proportion to the whole, that we now know to exist. Then we knew of no cases of buying and selling slaves among Methodists; but now we know it to be common. Then we knew of no local preachers, and deacons, and elders who held slaves; now they can be numbered by hundreds. Then a member of the Baltimore Conference was suspended for owning a slave through his wife; now several own slaves in this way, and one at least in his own right, and no notice is taken of it. Then there were no slaveholders in the Philadelphia Conference; now there are at least five in that Conference, even upon their own admission; and the Conference does not even express their disapproval. Neither did the presiding bishop exert himself to prevent the passage of their character, or to have the Conference disapprove of their conduct. We write this with pain. We helped to elect Bishop Ames, and personally have nothing against him. On the contrary, we like him personally, and would much rather, if we could, speak in his praise, than to write disapprovingly of his official acts. He has always treated us well, and we have no prejudices or ill feeling to gratify. With the feelings of a *Christian*, we trust, glowing in our bosom, and wishing him a thousand blessings, we are constrained to disapprove of his course at the Philadelphia Conference, and again to call the attention of the Methodist public to it. We owe it to the Anti-slavery cause; to the Methodist Episcopal Church; and to the honor of Methodist Episcopacy, if not to Bishop Ames and the slaveholding preachers themselves. "We love Cæsar much, but Rome more."

And now, as to what ought to be done:

I. A memorial should be got up, addressed to the Baltimore and Philadelphia Conferences, at least, and signed by thousands of travelling preachers in the Northern Conferences, praying them, for Christ's sake, for the peace and purity of the

Church, and the honor of their brethren in the Free States, as well as their own, to put away the accursed thing from among them; to appoint no more slaveholding class-leaders or stewards; to license no more slaveholding exhorters or local preachers; to elect no more to deacons' or elders' orders; and to enforce "the Discipline as it is" against all incumbents of any of these offices, who hold their positions, as all slaveholding officers do, in violation of the laws of the Church. And above all, should we entreat them to enforce the Discipline against all slaveholding members of their Conferences. Not only are the non-slaveholding members of the Border Conferences disgraced by the connection of their fellow-laborers with slavery, but we also, every Methodist preacher in the Church, even to the shores of Lake Erie and Ontario, and to the pine forests of Northern Maine. They owe it to us all, to roll away this reproach. And if appealed to in a memorial, respectful in language, and breathing the spirit of Christ, they *might* regard our earnest prayer.

II. If no favorable action is taken upon this subject by these Conferences, at their next sessions, then a complaint should be lodged against them at the next General Conference, by the anti-slavery men of that body, for *mal-administration*, in allowing their preachers to appoint men to official stations in the Church, who are not eligible to such posts; as, for instance, *slaveholders*, to the offices of leaders, stewards, exhorters, and local preachers. (See *Discipline*, page 213.) And above all, in electing slaveholding local preachers to deacons' and elders' orders, and allowing travelling preachers to hold slaves.

That the General Conference has the right to administer discipline upon the Annual Conference—at least, to reprove and censure, if not to disfellowship them—is beyond all question. Indeed, this right is virtually exercised by that body every four years, in reviewing the *Journals* of the several Annual Conferences, and sometimes disapproving or censuring their acts. This right is involved in adjudicating every *appeal* that comes before the General Conference.

Upon this subject Bishop Hedding says:

"That body [the General Conference] not only makes 'rules and regulations,' but administers discipline, first upon the bishops, and secondly on the Annual Conferences. * * *

"I said the General Conference administers discipline on the Annual Conferences. The General Conference constitutes these bodies, fixes their bounds, and authorizes them to act as Conferences; and therefore governs them. For this purpose they are required to bring a copy of the record of their proceedings to the General Conference for examination. And when it is remembered that some of these Annual Conferences are at a great distance from each other, that they are situated in countries of different manners, customs, and laws, it will be natural to suppose what is a fact, that there is a constant tendency, in some one or other of them, to go astray from Methodism. The unity and prosperity of the body then will depend, under God, in a great degree, on the watchful oversight the General Conference shall exercise over the Annual Conferences.

"But should an Annual Conference do wrong, what power has the General Conference to punish? Administer censure, reproof, and exhortation, as the case may require. But should the majority of an Annual Conference become heretical, or countenance immorality, what can the General Conference do? Other remedies may answer in some cases, yet I know of only *one* that can be constitutionally administered in all cases. That is, let the General Conference command the bishops to remove the corrupted majority of an Annual Conference to other parts of the work, and scatter them among other Annual Conferences, where they can be governed, and supply their places with better men from other Conferences.

"But such men would not go at the appointment of the bishop. Perhaps they would not personally; but their names, and their membership would go where they could be dealt with as their sins should deserve."—(*Discourse on the Administration of Discipline*, pp. 7, 25–27.)

This discourse was published in 1841, and had all the force of an official exposition of the Discipline. It was bound up with the Discipline in 1843, and was virtually endorsed by the General Conference of 1844, in approving of Bishop Hedding's official acts.

The part of the discourse above quoted was understood at the time as an intimation, that unless the anti-slavery men of New England kept pretty quiet, they might get transferred to Florida or Mississippi.

Now we suppose this doctrine will hold equally good as to slaveholding Conferences and preachers. And if the General Conference has authority to reprove and censure a slaveholding Conference, and does not do it, she becomes a tacit party to the crime, and endorses slaveholding by official members, local and travelling preachers, in the most effectual manner. The honor of the whole Church will therefore be involved in the course which the next General Conference takes, in regard to the Baltimore and Philadelphia Conferences. And unless they reform at their next sessions respectively, their administrative and moral apostasy should be formally brought before the next

General Conference, in the shape of a bill of charges and specifications.

III. The Committee on Episcopacy should investigate the public allegations of Dr. McFerrin, in regard to our bishops; and ascertain, as in the case of Bishop Andrew in 1844, which of the bishops, if any, are connected with slavery, and to what extent. And also, whether or not they have *knowingly* ordained either local or travelling ministers as deacons or elders, and to what extent; and to take such action as the results of their inquiries may demand. And if the Committee do not seem disposed to do their duty upon this delicate subject, it should be brought before the whole body, and made the duty of the committee by special resolution.

IV. The administration of Bishop Ames, at the Philadelphia Conference of March, 1858, should be thoroughly investigated. It has been publicly alleged that he decided that no man could be arrested in the examination of character before the Conference, except upon written charges and specifications—that he passed the character of several slaveholding preachers, knowing them to be such, and when under verbal arrest for slaveholding, *by episcopal prerogative*, and *without a vote of Conference!* It has also been alleged that he took a strong party stand with the slaveholders, speaking commendingly of one of them; and making remarks respecting the pertinency of the question, "Are you a slaveholder?" calculated to throw odium and ridicule upon the few anti-slavery men of the Conference, and which did have that effect.

All this and even more has been publicly alleged by responsible Methodist preachers. It is either true or false. If false, the persons so misrepresenting the facts in the case should be expelled from the Church. If true, the administration of the bishop concerned should be either approved or condemned. The honor of our Episcopacy and of the Church, as well as our future safety against erroneous decisions and unwarrantable prerogatives, require it. Even-handed justice should be meted out to every man alike, whether the humblest preacher in our ranks, or the most influential dignitary of the Church. For these and many other reasons the administration of Bishop Ames, at the Philadelphia Conference of 1858, should be religiously but thoroughly investigated.

V. The next General Conference should give some expression of its views in regard to the propriety of our bishops seeking to exert a controlling influence over the legislation of the Church. If the Episcopacy see fit to present an Address to each General Conference (a duty, by the way, that is nowhere required by the Discipline), it ought to be understood whether or not they are expected to inform the General Conference what they can or cannot do by way of legislation. The question is, should the executive authority of the Church seek to control or direct the legislative department? Should our bishops feel at liberty to forestall the action of the General Conference upon any subject, by volunteering their opinions, or faith, or doubts, or fears?

In 1844, when a bishop had gone into slaveholding, the Episcopacy endeavored to prevent action against him, by urging a postponement for four years; but the General Conference took their own view of the matter, and acted as they thought best. In 1856, the Episcopacy again interfered with pending legislation, in their Address at Indianapolis, by expressing their "strong doubts," whether the General Conference had a right to legislate slavery out of the Church. A majority of the body were indignant when that portion of the Address was read; and some talked courageously against it in private, for a day or two; but, with one exception, no man alluded to the "outrage" upon the floor of the Conference, and in hearing of the bishops. But the procedure gave general dissatisfaction throughout most of the Church. It was thought to be an unwarrantable interference, designed to shield slavery; and that this suspicion was not an uncharitable one, is proved by the fact, that *one* of the bishops, at least, has since said, that they (the bishops) supposed their opinion, thus expressed, would have the effect to prevent legislation against slavery; and that they put it into the Episcopal Address for that purpose!

Now if this is a prerogative of our Episcopacy, we have not a word to say, further than this: that we think their prerogatives should, in this respect, be curtailed. But if it is not proper for our bishops to bring their immense influence and authority to bear upon the legislation of the Church, especially to shield an overshadowing enormity, then the General Conference ought in some respectful and appropriate manner to indicate their views.

It is high time that a guard was set up at this point. "I am now going home," said the lamented J. B. FINLEY to us, just before the close of the last General Conference; "I am now going home, and shall never be at another General Conference. But I want you young men to knock that episcopal ordination out of the Discipline, or we are gone. I have seen that at this General Conference that I never expected to see, and it alarms me." And the "OLD CHIEF" paced the portico of the capitol backward and forward, as if deeply distressed in mind. These were the last words we ever heard from his lips; and we understood them to refer to the immense influence of the bishops, growing largely out of their third ordination, and the recent misuse of that influence, as he conceived, in interfering with the legislation of the Church.

As pertinent in this connection, we will here quote an extract from an article that appeared in *Zion's Herald*, for Oct. 28, 1857, over the signature of "MONITOR." Alluding to the article, Dr. Haven said: "The communication under this title is from one of the ablest men in the Church, and who holds one of the most responsible of its offices. Of course none will fail to read it." Whether rightfully or not, the article has generally been credited to Dr. WHEDON, editor of the *Methodist Quarterly Review;* and, if his, is certainly no disparagement to either his head or heart. He says:

"Again, this Border power may very seriously affect an Episcopacy. We know not by what charm they can accomplish it; but it is an imaginable idea that a Border overseership can assimilate to its own image an entire episcopal bench. Time was in bonny England when it was said that 'a Liberal promoted, became a Conservative in office.' A state of things is conceivable when the sure way to convert a man from abolitionism is to elect him bishop. We have heard of the cave of Trophonius, through which the man who passed was never seen again to smile. Anti-slavery fanciers have even now imagined that our Episcopacy can be a Trophonian cave, through which they have seen more than one once jovial abolitionist pass—and they have never since been able to catch one smile from beneath his mitred brow. There is a possibility for the episcopal sunshine to be selective and beam only upon pro-slavery objects; while its dark, withering night-side may shed damp and gloom over every anti-slavery point and personality. Episcopacy may utter speeches at our indignant Conferences which conservatism, that is, political conservatism, shall quote to the echo; may pass eulogies upon slaveholders scarce consistent with the tenor of our Discipline; may interpose at General Conference constitutional objections just at the crisis of action; may never be heard to utter one anti-slavery *clausula*, until forced to speak in self-defence in a foreign land. Such a sympathy may exist between the Border overseership and an Episcopacy, as that the latter may seem to become 'OVERSEERS over the Church of God in a sort of plantation sense. The Episcopacy we conceive to be an ornament, a crowning capital to the Church, giving it a majesty impressive upon the public mind; but sad is the case when it shall permanently cease to be the true representative, as well as the crown of the Church. Not long would the Church in such a case rest without seeking some method of restoring the harmony between the body and the head."

This is all supposition, of course, but when one states as *possible*, what has to some extent taken place already, the application is irresistible.

But letting the past go, we think it is due to its own honor, as well as to good order and peace among ourselves, that the next General Conference give some expression of their views upon this subject; for if our bishops should chance to become pro-slavery, as every one will admit to be possible, and should bring all their immense influence and patronage to bear upon successive General Conferences to prevent legislation against slavery, we might weep and pray and toil in vain, for a pure Church, till the end of time.

VI. The present chapter on slavery, Discipline, page 212, should be stricken out, every word of it, except the title, and the first four lines. With this exception, the whole chapter is eminently pro-slavery. The *fifth* answer to the question, "What shall be done for the extirpation of the evil of slavery," is, that bishops may employ colored preachers; as if it required a special dispensation to allow a colored man to preach! The *fourth* answer conforms our treatment of colored preachers and official members to "the usages of the country." The *third* fully allows "all our members," to hold "their slaves," provided they teach them to read, &c. The *second* allows a travelling preacher to own slaves, if the State where he lives will not allow of emancipation; for he is to emancipate "if it be practicable," by the State laws. If, therefore, there be no emancipation laws, then he may hold his slaves still, according to the Discipline. It does not require him to liberate his slaves, if need be, by letting them go to a free State, but, on the contrary, the Discipline is subjugated to the iniquitous laws and usages of the slave States. And the *first* answer allows official members to hold slaves to any extent, provided the State laws are only right. But none of these provisos cover the slaveholders now in the Methodist Episcopal Church, as already shown on page 56.

Such being the general character of the present chapter on Slavery, we regard it as a disgrace to the Church to have it remain upon our statute-book another hour; and we earnestly pray that as early as May 15, 1860, it may disappear from the pages of the Discipline *forever!*

VII. In place of the cancelled pro-slavery chapter, the General Conference should insert a clear and effectual prohibitory and extirpatory law. It should at last *do something* for the "EXTIRPATION" of slavery. This will require the two following provisions:

1st. *That no slaveholder shall ever hereafter be admitted into the Methodist Episcopal Church;* and,

2d. *That those now in the Church—ministers, official members, and private members alike—shall be required to either liberate their slaves or retire from the Church; or else shall be excluded from it.*

A brief, well-guarded, and unambiguous law, to this effect, inserted in place of what we now have in the chapter, is, in our view, *what* we want, and *all* we want. We also regard direct legislation in the chapter, as the only legitimate and safe process of legislating slaveholding out of the Church.

As to the idea of some, that we may prohibit the future admission of slaveholders, but ought not to Discipline those now in the Church, it does not accord with our ideas of right, or of good policy. If a slaveholder is too bad a man to be *admitted* into the Church, those already in are too bad to be allowed to *stay* in it. It would be a great piece of inconsistency, it seems to us, to keep from ten to twenty thousand slaveholders in the Church, till they die off and go to —— (we dare not say *Heaven*, and so leave the reader to fill the blank as he chooses), while we shut the door in the face of five or ten thousand more who wish to come in. It would be another moral compromise; and like all compromises with sin, would corrupt and curse us. It would rob the prohibitory legislation of all its moral force, and make the Methodist Episcopal Church the laughing-stock of slaveholders, as well as of all the Churches in the land. With such a statutory toleration of slavery, it *would never die out*—NEVER! The administration on the Border would rectify the inconsistency of the Discipline, not by putting slaveholders out, but by letting others in; and slavery would be perpetuated in the Methodist Episcopal Church for a hundred years to come.

With the fear that such legislation would be *ex post facto* we have no sympathy. The General Rules, professedly based upon the Bible, and the teachings of the Holy Spirit in truly awakened hearts, forbid doing harm; doing to others as we would not they should do to us; doing what we know is not for the glory of God, &c. They either thereby forbid slaveholding, or they do not. If they do not, then slaveholding is no "harm;" is what we would have others do to us; is written by the Spirit of God in the heart, and is for the glory of God. We ought, therefore, to encourage and not to legislate against it. But if the General Rules forbid it, as much as they do piracy, or arson, or sodomy, which they nowhere mention by name, then we have had law against slaveholding all along, and before the fact; and the proposed extirpatory law would not be *ex post facto*.

We contend that *by the fundamental law of the Church*—the General Rules—non-slaveholding has been a condition of membership from the beginning, and is still. It is the *administration* on the Border, and not the law of the Church, that has filled her with slaveholders. "If that is Methodism," said Rev. J. B. Finley, after hearing Abel Stevens' speech in the last General Conference; "if that is Methodism, then I am not and never have been a Methodist." And even the conservative Peter Cartwright said, "I don't believe that doctrine. I have always told them that every slaveholder in the Methodist Church was there in violation of the Discipline." This is the true view of the case, so far as the Constitution of the Church is concerned.

On the other hand, to concede that a law excluding slaveholders now in the Church, would be *ex post facto*, is to admit that they are *lawfully* in the Church; or, in other words, that *the very Constitution of the Church* protects them in holding slaves. If this be so, then the same Constitution guarantees membership to all slaveholders that apply for admission, and a merely prohibitory law would be unconstitutional. The whole question turns upon the claim set up at the last General Conference—whether or not we are *constitutionally*, as well as administratively, a slaveholding Church. If we *are*, we cannot legislate in the chapter at all, even to prohibit the future admission of slaveholders, till we change the Constitution; and if we *are not*, then an excluding law is in harmony with our fundamental law, and would not be *ex post facto*.

We are opposed, therefore, to a temporizing legislation that shall give to some 15,000 slaveholders a life-lease of the Methodist Episcopal Church. Heaven knows we have had enough of them, and suffered enough by them! And whether we succeed or fail; or, if we succeed, whether the Border regard the law, or nullify it or secede, we should attempt to make the Discipline RIGHT, whatever may be the consequences. Even if it were true that, by management and scheming, slavery had got an advantage over freedom and moral purity, in the disciplinary framework of the Church, even then, let what might follow, we would have Christ's Church tear down the black flag of slavery, and run up, and nail to the mast, the white flag of liberty, holiness, and peace. We cannot admit that the Discipline is of higher authority than the Bible. We should obey God rather than man, though a thousand Disciplines were torn into fragments. Such is our moral philosophy.

But we are brought to no such alternative. The fundamental law of the Church, built upon the Bible, is in harmony with it; and all we want now is consistent and thorough statutory legislation in the chapter on slavery, carrying out and applying the pure and holy principles of the Constitution. And this will we have, if God permit.

There are two other modes of legislation proposed, to which we ought, perhaps, to give some attention. The first is, to append a note to the General Rule, explaining it according to its original design, as opposed to all slaveholding. Next to direct legislation in the chapter, we regard this as the best measure. But we believe it liable to more and weightier objections than can be urged against legislation in the chapter; and that it will be far less likely to succeed.

1. It virtually concedes that we have no right to legislate in the chapter. Else why not go there at once, and not go to tinkering the Constitution, by tacking an explanatory note to it?

2. If it could be urged with effect in 1856, that we could not condemn slaveholding in the chapter by a majority vote, because it would be "equivalent" to a change of the General

Rules, what would be said of appending an explanatory note to the Constitution, without the constitutional process of amendment? Would not the appending of such a note to the General Rule, be much more like "altering" the General Rule, than legislation in the statute-book, entirely away from the Constitution? We think it would; and that it would not only meet with less favor and stronger opposition than direct legislation, on that account, but would leave us far more exposed in case of another Southern secession, and a second appeal to the civil tribunals.

3. This note process looks too much to us like dodging the issue now raised, and which we ought openly and fairly to meet, viz., the constitutional question. If the Constitution protects slaveholders, then we ought not to thrust at them by a note of interpretation appended to it. It is, it seems to us, an unmanly way of condemning them.

We wish to condemn all slaveholding *openly* and *fairly*, and before the light of the sun. It is only from the belief that the Constitution is anti-slavery, that we can tolerate the idea of appending a note to the Rule for a moment. And even then we don't like it. It is less *frank* and *manly* it seems to us, than it would be to put an effectual prohibitory law into the chapter on slavery. Still, we should reluctantly vote for it, if in the next General Conference and we could get nothing better.

So much for what is called the "Interpretation policy," to which several of the Northwestern Conferences have this year (1858) committed themselves.

Another plan is that advocated by ABEL STEVENS and others, at the last General Conference, viz., to change the General Rule on slavery, if any thing, by getting a vote of three fourths of all the preachers present and voting in the several Annual Conferences; and two thirds of the succeeding General Conference—this being the vote required to change any of the General Rules. The original ground for this change was, that the General Rule *protects* slaveholders; and the Church cannot legally disfranchise them, except by an alteration of her Constitution. This doctrine, however, is now almost universally repudiated throughout the non-slaveholding Conferences. And yet, though the original ground of the argument for such a change is repudiated, there are those, though a minority we are confident, who think it best to attempt to change the General Rule on slavery. To this attempt we are most decidedly opposed, and for the following reasons:

1. It is *not necessary* in order to legislate slavery out of the Church. Few, indeed, can now be found who do not repudiate the doctrine, that the Constitution of the Methodist Episcopal Church protects slaveholders, and must therefore be changed, as the only legal mode of legislating against them. On the contrary, even most of those who advocate this measure, admit that we have a perfect right to exclude all slavery from the Church by direct legislation. We are not, therefore, driven to this mode of procedure by any necessity in the case.

2. Such an attempt would be, in our view, a virtual concession of the constitutional argument; for, disclaim as much as we may, the potent interrogatory would be, "If you did not feel that the Constitution was in your way, why did you try to alter it?" And it would not be a sufficient reply to say, "It was not sufficiently explicit, and we wished to make it clear and unambiguous." Such an answer of itself, to a large extent, yields the constitutional argument as against us; thus not only giving the pro-slavery party in the Church a moral vantage-ground to which they are not entitled, but reflecting upon the moral character of the Church, and upon the fair fame of our fathers of 1784, who put the present Rule into the Discipline. Far better, we think, to stand erect upon the immutable truth, that the Constitution of the Methodist Episcopal Church is now and always has been against all slaveholding, and then condemn it afresh in 1860 by statute law, as we have a perfect right to do.

3. At the very best, to attempt to reach slavery by altering the Constitution, is to give every pro-slavery man the strength of three anti-slavery men. It requires three votes *for* the measure to one against it, to change the General Rules. Thus one man in Baltimore Conference will balance three in Wisconsin or Genesee, as the Southern slaveholder votes for his slaves, and thus keeps control of the General Government. Now if this was *our only legal course*, we might be induced to try it, if it did not cost the Church too much of character, and was not utterly hopeless; but when it is so generally conceded that we have a perfect right to legislate in the chapter on slavery, where a simple majority of the General Conference can

enact an extirpatory law; we cannot see the wisdom of trying what is, at best, a dubious experiment; and must succeed, if at all, with the utmost difficulty. Why, in a matter of so much moment, should we abandon a certainty for an uncertainty? That the General Conference have a *right* to pass a law, by a simple majority vote, excluding all slaveholders from the Church, even Dr. Bond admitted; and that this *can* be done by the next General Conference, very few doubt. But that the Constitution can be changed by a vote of three fourths of the members of all the Annual Conferences, and two thirds of the next General Conference, not one in a hundred believes. Why, then, should it be undertaken?

4. We take the still higher ground, that *the change of the General Rule, in a way clearly to prohibit all slaveholding, is, under existing circumstances*, MORALLY IMPOSSIBLE. And for this opinion we will submit our reasons. Let us first look over the several Conferences, and see what kind of a vote will be necessary in order to change the General Rule:

CONFERENCES.	Whole No. of Preachers.	For a change.	Against a change.	CONFERENCES.	Whole No. of Preachers.	For a change.	Against a change.
Baltimore	180	10	170	Upper Iowa	139	139	
East Baltimore	199	10	189	Providence	144	144	
Philadelphia	234	20	214	New England	165	165	
New Jersey	119	10	109	East Maine	101	101	
Newark	132	15	117	Maine	125	125	
Western Virginia	97		97	New Hampshire	108	108	
Kentucky	24		24	Vermont	81	81	
Arkansas	19		19	Black River	203	203	
Missouri	65		65	Oneida	184	184	
Oregon	57	20	37	Genesee	122	122	
California	85	15	70	East Genesee	185	185	
Pittsburgh	208	59	149	Erie	205	205	
Cincinnati	199	152	47	Ohio	167	167	
Kansas and Nebraska	48	40	8	North Ohio	145	145	
New York	251	31	220	Delaware	114	114	
New York East	182	100	82	Michigan	123	123	
Wyoming	101	101		Detroit	127	127	
Troy	243	243		Rock River	176	176	
Indiana	144	144		Wisconsin	142	142	
Southeast Indiana	125	125		West Wisconsin	94	94	
North Indiana	106	106		Minnesota	76	76	
Northwest Indiana	104	104		Peoria	132	132	
Illinois	206	206					
Southern Illinois	146	146		Total	6472	4855	1617
Iowa	140	140					

In the preceding table, the number of preachers is taken from the Minutes for 1858; and allowing forty votes for Kansas and one hundred for New York East, and every vote in the remaining thirty-one Conferences, we get a majority of one! The figures stand thus:

Whole number of voters....................	6,472
Three fourths, necessary to a change.........	4,854
For a change, as per above..................	4,855
Votes to spare............................	1

But no such vote can ever be obtained; for,

(1.) Great numbers in all the free Conferences believe the attempt unnecessary and suicidal, and will either vote against it, or not vote at all. A large majority of the five Conferences in Central New York, as well as many others, take this view of the matter, and will not be willing to abet or countenance the project in any way. They regard it as a pro-slavery diversion, inaugurated by a renegade from the ranks of anti-slavery, and only calculated to defeat all anti-slavery legislation.

(2.) If any Northern Conference, voting upon such a proposition, fails to *count* and *record* their vote, the entire vote will be lost in the canvas. Several Conferences in the Northwest have recently voted in this way, declaring their vote "unanimous," but by not recording the number voting, throwing away the whole. And so it will be next year, if the experiment is tried. Whole Northern Conferences will lose their votes, by informality in voting. But the Border will never lose a vote by any such omission.

(3.) In order to succeed, there must be a vote of three fourths, of all the preachers present and voting, in favor of *the same amendment*. Now there were four different propositions in the field in 1855, viz., those known respectively as the Troy, Wisconsin, Ohio, and Erie resolutions. They were all presented at the same time, and as some Conferences preferred one and some another, the effect was precisely as if a political party were to get up *four candidates*, as the means of defeating the opposite party. By this division the vote was so meagre for each, that the bishops never reported it to the General Conference (as we think they should have done), but simply said in their Episcopal Address, "we believe no one of these resolutions received the constitutional majority," &c. We presume not, nor *one fifth* of the requisite majority; and if the bishops had reported the vote on these resolutions, it would have shown the utter folly of all such attempts, and exploded forever the Stevens policy of changing the Constitution to get at slavery.

But as it was in 1855, so will it be again in 1859. There are already two different propositions in the hands of the bishops, to divide the votes of the North, viz., one from the New Hampshire Conference, and another from the Cincinnati; and there will be several more, no doubt, before the final and official vote is called for. By this means the Northern vote will be divided into fragments; while the Border, who want no change, have simply to vote against them all, and they have saved every vote they cast.

It is useless to say that the Northern Conferences *can* agree upon one and the same proposition. It is morally impossible. Suppose, for instance, the Oneida Conference were to a man in favor of *some* change of the General Rule; and the presiding bishop should present the New Hampshire proposition, to make the Rule forbid "the buying, selling, or holding of a human being as property;" and also the Cincinnati amendment, "the buying or selling of men, women, or children, or the holding of them with an intention to use them as slaves;" who does not see that these two propositions would divide the vote of the Conference? If we voted for either personally, we should vote for the first; for we regard the second as actually modifying the Constitution of the Church in favor of slaveholding. And so with other propositions that will be presented. Whatever the Conferences *might* do, by way of agreeing upon a single proposition, it is enough to know that they *will not* so agree; and for this reason alone, if for no other, the project would be defeated.

(4.) Our bishops, as a whole, are opposed to any change or law that will put slavery out of the Church. For this we have seen what may be regarded as reasons in the preceding pages. It may be that two of them are not much opposed; but four of the six are strongly opposed to any such change; and so far as they may see fit to exert their influence, personally or otherwise, will oppose the change of the Rule. And that they do not think it improper to use their great influence to defeat legislation which they do not approve, is attested, not only by their opening Address at Indianapolis in 1856, but also by the private labors of some of them to the same end. The plan may, therefore, be expected to encounter whatever influence the bishops may see fit to exert, both in the cabinets of the several Conferences, and by personal intercourse with the preachers. But there will be no need of *their* opposition in order to secure a failure.

Now taking all these things into the account, who can believe that the thirty-one Conferences in the table, after New York East, will cast a solid vote for any one of three or four different propositions that will be presented to them? Who can believe that one half of the numbers credited to these Conferences will ever be realized? The first twelve Conferences will vote nearly solid against *all* changes, and can cast 1419 votes; while the remaining thirty-five Conferences will never cast 2000 votes in favor of any one proposition. Our conclusion, therefore, is, that *if the experiment is tried* (as we pray that it may not be), we shall not get within A THOUSAND VOTES of enough to change the General Rule! By this estimate, which we first made and published in December, 1857, we are willing to abide till time and figures shall demonstrate its general correctness in the autumn of 1859.

(5.) A change of the General Rule being morally impossible, we are opposed to any *attempts* to do it. In 1856, the previous attempt and failure to get a three fourth vote in the Annual Conferences, was used even by the Episcopacy as an implied admission that *that* was the only constitutional way to legislate against slavery. And now, if we try again and fail, as we inevitably must, we have shut ourselves up to this alternative: either not to legislate in the chapter, and have nothing done on the subject; or to legislate there, after having twice tried in vain to change the Constitution; thus disparaging the anti-slavery cause; dampening the energies of anti-slavery men by a mortifying defeat; and, in the event of a secession on the Border, and consequent litigation, giving to the pro-slavery party an immense advantage over us in the courts of justice.

For these and other reasons, we say, *make no attempt whatever to change the Constitution of the Methodist Episcopal Church.* It is right enough as it is. All we want is to get rid of our pro-slavery *chapter* on slavery; get a good strong extirpatory law in its place; and then look after the *administration* in our slave territory.

Let us now see *why* these desirable objects should be effected, especially the enactment of an extirpatory law in the chapter on slavery.

CHAPTER IX.

WHY ALL SLAVEHOLDING SHOULD BE EXCLUDED FROM THE METHODIST EPISCOPAL CHURCH.

There are many and weighty reasons why the next General Conference should settle this great question forever, so far as the law of the Church is concerned.

I. *Slaveholding is a great moral wrong.* We profess to be Christians, and ought not, therefore, to be a body of oppressors and man-stealers. Slaveholding is the fruitful parent of injustice, cruelty, adultery, fornication, and murder; and unless the house of God is to be made a den of thieves, *slavery* ought, therefore, to be driven beyond her pale. We, as a denomination, owe it to our common Christianity; to our professions of moral purity; to the name and memory of Wesley, and Coke, and Asbury, to wash our hands of this foul iniquity, and restore the Methodist Episcopal Church to her original position and purity. We owe it to Christ, whose name we bear as professed Christians, to rise up and drive all, who, in violation of every principle of justice and humanity, will claim property in man, out of the kingdom of God.

II. *We owe it to our Christian brethren in Europe.* It is but a few months since an appeal was addressed to all the Protestant Churches in this country, informing us that "scandal now covers the American name and glory," and infidelity is greatly strengthened in Europe on account of the connection of the American Church with slavery.

This address was signed by *five thousand four hundred and forty-three* names, including the names of the pastors, elders, and deacons of all the "*Reformed*" Churches of France; the pastors and elders of all the evangelical Churches constituted upon the Augsburg Confession; and the pastors and other officers of all the independent Churches, *i. e.*, those Congregational, Presbyterian, Methodist, and Baptist Churches that are independent of the State. The address asserts that infidels and all opposers to religion in Europe are constantly pressing them with such objections to the Bible as this:

"Protestantism," they say, and "SLAVERY agree wonderfully well. In the United States this odious institution numbers many Christians among its advocates; they preach and pray in its behalf, they labor to extend its territory. And this slavery, for which they thus act, is the selling of families by retail; the breaking up of marriage; the yearly recruiting of the market with men, women, and children, picked one by one from the plantations of Virginia and Kentucky; it is, in short, a monstrous thing, not merely revolting to pious minds, but at variance with the first elements of humanity. Nevertheless, the Protestants of America accept this state of things; they deem it in accordance with the Gospel, and the Protestants of Europe undoubtedly think as they do, or they would have vented their feelings in one strong outcry of grief and disapprobation!"

The following are the closing paragraphs of the address:

"Doubly united to you as Christians and as Frenchmen, can we err in sending you this utterance, whose sincerity you cannot suspect? Have we presumed too far in believing that this unanimous appeal from sister Churches would not in vain be cast into the scales where the destiny of American Christianity is now being weighed?

"May the spirit of the God of Truth and of Love be with you in this fearful crisis, and rest upon you, your Churches, and your country!

"Your affectionate Brethren in Jesus Christ.

"June 1, 1857."

[*Here follow the signatures.*]

Thus, while we are tolerating this great sin in the Churches here, we are strengthening the hands of the wicked against Christianity, not only here, but as far as the disgraceful fact is known. Is it right to put such a weapon into the hands of French and English infidels, with which to fight our fellow-laborers across the water? We think not; and that for their sake also, we should exclude all slaveholders from the Methodist Episcopal Church.

III. *The position taken by several other branches of the Church of Christ in America* should stir us up to do our duty in this respect.

1. The FRIENDS (or Quakers, as they are sometimes called) have long borne an unequivocal and weighty testimony against this great sin. They not only have no slaveholders among them, and will have none, but many of them will not use a

pound of sugar or rice, or a yard of cotton cloth, produced by the unpaid labor of slaves.

2. The FREE WILL BAPTIST CHURCH, a zealous and devoted body of Christians, have no fellowship with slaveholders.

3. The UNITED BRETHREN IN CHRIST, a growing and excellent denomination, most numerous in the West, have, if we are rightly informed, no fellowship with slaveholders.

4. The ASSOCIATE and ASSOCIATE REFORMED PRESBYTERIAN Churches, minor branches of the Presbyterian family in the United States, entered into a formal union, by which they became one body, at a recent meeting in Alleghany City, Pa. In this union they assumed the true Scriptural position of no fellowship with slaveholders.

5. The WESLEYAN METHODIST CONNECTION, in this country, have no fellowship with slaveholders.

6. The CONGREGATIONAL CHURCHES of America, a vigorous and growing people, have no fellowship with slaveholders.

7. Prior to 1844 the Baptist Churches in this country were united in what was called the Baptist General Convention. In November of that year, the Alabama Baptist State Convention addressed a letter to the General Board at Boston, demanding an avowal, "that slaveholders are eligible and entitled, equally with non-slaveholders, to all the privileges and immunities of their several unions," &c. To this the Board at Boston nobly replied, that they would not appoint a slaveholder as a missionary, nor in any other way "be a party to any arrangement that would imply approbation of slavery." This caused the South to secede, like our Southern secession of 1845, and the present Northern Baptist Churches have no fellowship with slaveholders.*

8. The REFORMED PROTESTANT DUTCH CHURCH, at the session of its General Synod, held in New York, Oct., 1855, refused to admit the Classis of North Carolina (which answers to one of our Annual Conferences), on the ground of their connection with slavery; thus taking the position of no fellowship with slaveholders.

9. The NEW SCHOOL PRESBYTERIAN CHURCH have also purged themselves from this great iniquity. At the meeting of the General Assembly, held in Cleveland, May, 1857, the subject

* Facts for Baptist Churches, pp. 104–107.

of slavery in the Church was brought before the body by memorials from different parts of the country, and a report was presented, affirming that "the Presbyterian Church in these United States has, from the beginning, maintained an attitude of decided opposition to the institution of slavery," and proving it by abundant and conclusive evidence from the records of the body. The report deplores the fact, that "the Presbytery of Lexington, South, have given official notice to us, that a number of ministers and ruling elders, as well as many church-members in their connection, hold slaves 'from principle,' and 'of choice,' 'believing it to be according to Bible right,'" &c.; and finally proceeds to reaffirm its original doctrine, and to "bear testimony" against the sin of slaveholding. This excellent report was adopted by a vote of 169 to 26;* whereupon the delegates from slaveholding presbyteries protested against the action, as follows:

"We, the undersigned Southern Ministers and Ruling Elders, protest against the present decision of the General Assembly.

"We protest—Because, while past General Assemblies have asserted, that the system of slavery is wrong, they have heretofore affirmed, that the slaveholder was so controlled by State laws, obligations of guardianship, and humanity, that he was, as thus situated, without censure or odium as the master. This averment in the testimony of past Assemblies has so far satisfied the South, as to make it unnecessary to do more than protest against the mere anti-slavery part of such testimony.

"We protest then, now, That the present act of the Assembly is such an assertion of the sin of slavery, as degrades the whole Southern Church—an assertion without authority from the word of God, or the organic law of the Presbyterian body.

"We protest, that such action is, under present conditions, the virtual exscinding of the South, whatever be the motives of those who vote the deed.

"We protest, that such indirect excision is unrighteous, oppressive, uncalled for—the exercise of usurped power—destructive of the unity of our branch of the Church—hurtful to the North and the South—and adding to the peril of the union of these United States.

"Fred. A. Ross, Robt. P. Rhea,
Jas. G. Hamner, F. R. Gray,
Isaac W. K. Handy, M. S. Shuck,
Gideon S. White, W. E. Caldwell,
George W. Hutchins, E. A. Carson,
George Painter, R. M. Morrison,
Henry Mathews, Robert McLain,
John F. Chester, A. J. Modie,
J. V. Barks, Peachy R. Grattan,
J. B. Logan, Thomas H. Cleland,
C. M. Atkinson, Archer C. Dickerson."

---

* It is worthy of note that every delegate sent up to this General Assembly from the Presbytery of New York, was an abolitionist, and voted for the report. They

A committee was appointed to answer this protest, who reported as follows:

"In reply to the protest against the action taken by the Assembly on the subject of slavery, the Assembly make the following remarks:

"1. The present action of the Assembly on this subject is in perfect harmony with the testimonies of former Assemblies, and consists chiefly in a reaffirmation of those testimonies. The General Assembly has never 'affirmed that the slaveholder was so controlled by State laws, obligations of guardianship and humanity, that he was, as thus situated, without censure or odium as the master.' It has only conceded, that certain exceptional cases may exist, such as are defined in the resolutions of the Assembly of 1850, and approved by this Assembly.

"2. We see nothing in the present action which is unconstitutional, or which 'degrades,' or even reflects upon, any portion of the Southern Church, which still abides by the old doctrine of the Presbyterian Church in relation to this subject.

"3. With respect to the complaint, 'that such action is, under present conditions, the virtual exscinding of the South,' the Assembly observe, that no such excision is intended, and we cannot perceive that it is in any wise involved even by remote implication. We have simply reaffirmed the established views of the Presbyterian Church on the subject of slavery, and distinctly condemned the new and counter doctrines which have been declared and defended by some within our bounds.

"4. With regard to the allegation, that our action in this case is 'unrighteous, oppressive, uncalled for,' usurpatory and destructive of great interests, we need only say, that it rests on the groundless assumption, that this action is an 'indirect excision' of the South. If our Southern brethren shall break the unity of the Church, because we stand by our former position, as in duty bound, the responsibility for the consequences will not rest on the Assembly."

This reply having been adopted, Dr. Ross and his followers proceeded at once to prepare for secession, which they consummated at a convention held in Richmond, Va., in September following. What a striking resemblance between this case and that of our own Church in 1844—the action, the Protest, the Reply, the Convention, &c. Dr. Ross led off one, Dr. Smith the other. One convention was held in Richmond, Va., and the other in Louisville, Ky.; and both factions have gone headlong into slavery, as a most holy Bible institution.

Still further, both factions are already smitten with mildew and decay. The Methodist Episcopal Church South, during the unprecedented revivals of the past year, have had only about 12,000 increase, while the Methodist Episcopal Church proper has had an increase of some 100,000. The Southern

---

were Ed. F. Hatfield, D.D., Samuel D. Burchard, D.D., and T. McLaughlin, D.D., ministers; and Messrs. Roe Lockwood, J. C. Hines, and Wm. C. Foote, Esqs., laymen. What a contrast with the delegates sent from the New York Conference to Indianapolis, in 1856!

papers scarce one of them pay their expenses, and their Book Concern must inevitably die, so soon as they cease to draw their thousands annually from the Book Concern at New York —the hard-earned money of freemen taken by unrighteous judgments to support oppression. But it will not be long. And ten years will leave scarce a vestige of a periodical or book-room in the South, to advocate and uphold slavery. "So may all thy enemies perish, O Lord!"

Previously to the preceding action of the New School General Assembly, the American Home Missionary Society, sustained mainly by New School Presbyterians, had felt themselves called upon to take action in regard to the question of appropriating funds to build up slaveholding Churches; and, on the 22d of December, 1856, the executive committee passed the following without a dissenting vote:

> "*Resolved*, That in the disbursement of the funds committed to their trust, the Committee will not grant aid to Churches containing slaveholding members, unless evidence be furnished that the relation is such as, in the judgment of the Committee, is justifiable, for the time being, in the peculiar circumstances in which it exists."

This decision was pronounced "unconstitutional," and "oppressive," and almost every thing else that was bad, by the advocates of slavery; but the committee adhered inflexibly to their purpose, and the Church and the public have fully borne them out in it. They were called "troubles of Israel," but they charged it back upon *slavery*, and to this day stand upon that exalted Christian platform, with perhaps this improvement, that practically they do nothing with their missionary funds, to gather slaveholders into the New School Presbyterian Church. What a contrast with *our* wretched pro-slavery policy of pouring out some $8000 a year, upon a few puny Conferences in slave territory in the Southwest!

Thus the New School Presbyterian Church has purged itself from slavery, and maintained its honor and Christian character; and it never stood so fair in the public estimation, or was half as prosperous, as it is now. They have done RIGHT, and have favor with God and with all good men.

So ought we to have done in 1856. But as we were divided and foiled by the slave power, acting through various mediums, and upon the hopes and fears of delegates; we ought, by the help of God, to rally in 1860, and place upon the brow of slavery the brand of outlawry and infamy, whatever may be the temporary consequences. If the Border "flare up" and secede, as Dr. Smith and his followers did in 1855, or as Dr. Ross and his fellow-slaveholders did in 1857, "let them go, and joy go with them." "We have delivered our souls."

10. Even the UNIVERSALISTS and UNITARIANS of the land have put us to shame in regard to American slavery. Time after time have they taken action against it, and they are known and read of all men as opposed to oppression.

The Old School Presbyterian Church, the Roman Catholic, and the Protestant Episcopal Church, are the only Northern pro-slavery Churches, the Methodist Episcopal Church excepted, in all these Free States. These are, if possible, worse off than we are; as they are not only full of slaveholders, both in the ministry and private membership, but they utterly ignore the subject, and are resolved to do nothing to redeem and purify themselves forever hereafter. With the exception of here and there a TYNG in the Protestant Episcopal Church, these clergy are all crying "Peace! peace!!" while slavery is rioting unrebuked in their midst.

Now look at our position as a Church in the light of these facts. See in what company we place ourselves. Let us range the anti-slavery and pro-slavery Northern Churches in parallel columns, that our shame may be the more apparent:

Anti-slavery Churches.	*Slave-holding Churches.*
1. FRIENDS, or QUAKERS.	1. OLD SCHOOL PRESBYTERIAN.
2. FREE-WILL BAPTISTS.	2. PROTESTANT EPISCOPAL.
3. UNITED BRETHREN.	3. ROMAN CATHOLIC.
4. ASSOCIATE PRESBYTERIAN.	4. METHODIST EPIS. CHURCH!!
5. WESLEYAN METHODISTS.	
6. ORTHODOX CONGREGATIONAL.	
7. GENERAL BAPTISTS.	
8. REF'D PROT. DUTCH CHURCH.	
9. NEW SCHOOL PRESBYTERIAN.	
10. UNITARIAN.	
11. UNIVERSALISTS!	

This is a faithful representation of the position of the several denominations in America, in regard to the great evil of slavery. Thus *we* stand to this day, as a denomination, the Church of WESLEY, and FLETCHER, and COKE, and ASBURY—the Church of free grace and full salvation—the Church of itinerancy, and class-meetings, and revivals, among the abettors and upholders of SLAVERY! What Methodist can look upon this humiliating fact for a moment, and not blush for his Church and for our common Christianity?

In view, therefore, of the noble examples set us by other denominations in this country, we say, let slavery be extirpated from the Methodist Episcopal Church in 1860. Let her stand up, henceforward, with the Baptist, and New School Presbyterian, and Wesleyan, and Congregational, and Reformed Dutch Churches, bearing aloft the white banner of FREEDOM, and with garments unspotted by the foul stain of oppression.

IV. *Such a course is due to our common country.* If slavery continues, it will yet ruin the North American Republic. This is now coming to be seen and felt more and more. And the pro-slavery Churches are this day the strongest bulwarks of slavery in the nation. Had all the Churches and ministers done their duty from the first, there would not have been a slave in the United States to-day—not one. And if they combine their testimony, even the Northern Churches, against this iniquity, it will do more than millions of gold to abolish slavery in the nation, and thus save our beloved Republic from utter dissolution. But our influence hitherto has not tended to the abolition of slavery.

Rev. DANIEL DE VINNE, of the New York Conference, who has probably seen as much of slavery in our Church as any Methodist preacher in the free States, sums up his observations in the following language:

> "We deplore the present position of our Church; and in view of all the ground, having travelled fifteen thousand miles in slaveholding States, having visited, perhaps, a thousand plantations, and having conversed freely with Methodist slaves and slaveholders, we must here record our solemn and religious testimony, that in our opinion the influence of the Methodist Episcopal Church, as administered for the last thirty years, has been unfavorable to the emancipation of slavery, either in our Church or in our country. For we fully believe, that 'the plea of necessity—the plea of certain circumstances,' and other excuses for the continuance of slavery in the Church, have done vastly more to uphold this enormous evil among us, than any direct advocacy of it could have possibly done. And we say this in sorrow, for we would not unnecessarily utter one word in opposition to the expressed opinions of our chief ministers, whose judgment, in all other respects, we highly appreciate."—(*Pamphlet*, p. 6.)

These things ought not so to be. The CHURCH should be the light of the world and the salt of the earth. She should be just and patriotic, and should do all she can to bless the State and perpetuate an efficient and Christian government. As we love our country, therefore, and wish her well, the powerful Methodist Episcopal Church, with her six thousand travelling preachers, and seven thousand local preachers, and nine hundred thousand members, and six hundred thousand Sunday-school scholars, and twenty colleges and universities, and sixty-five seminaries, and twenty periodicals,—this powerful Church should now wheel into line with the evangelical Churches of the country. She would be, in the great political and moral conflict now waging in this nation, like the battalions of Blucher upon the plains of Waterloo. Let us come to our place, then, we say, for "God and our native land."

V. *The movement now in progress, even in monarchical Europe*, should impel the *Churches* of America, especially, one and all, to take decided ground against slavery. At midnight on the 31st day of August, 1834—now a quarter of a century ago—England emancipated all the slaves in her West India possessions, some 800,000 souls. Then her poets could sing—

> "Slaves cannot breathe in England;
> The moment that their lungs receive our air,
> That moment they are free!"

And so it has been ever since, not only in England, but in her West India possessions, and in Canada, and wherever her proud ensign waves in the breezes of heaven. Her lion wears no chains, while our eagle, that glorious symbol of liberty, is fettered and degraded by the dark chains of slavery.

Russia, with her cold, formal Christianity, and her teeming millions of slaves, is moving rapidly in the work of emancipation. Twenty years will not find a slave in all the Russian dominions! Turkey, with only the religion of the false prophet, is fast tending to the universal freedom of her subjects. Portugal has recently abolished slavery in all her foreign dependencies; and even Spain, if ever Cuba should be fillibustered or purchased from her, and annexed to the United States, would at once abolish what little slavery would remain in her dominions. We should then stand alone in our glory as a model republic, with millions of slaves in her bosom! And all born "free and equal!" "Hail, Columbia! happy land!"

Unless, therefore, we wish to rivet the chains of slavery more and more, both upon the Church and nation, while even the old governments of Europe are proclaiming liberty to their captives, it is a duty which the Methodist Episcopal Church owes *to our country*, to arise, though it be at the eleventh hour, and throw her testimony and her influence into the scale of liberty.

VI. *Slavery is keeping thousands out of the Methodist Episcopal Church every year*, who are Christians, and love our doctrines and economy, and but for that great wrong, would gladly seek a home with us,—persons, too, of the highest intellectual and moral character and social position.

"Our connection with slavery," says the Rev. Mr. De Vinne, "is repelling thousands from our Church, and it is continually insulting the moral sense of hundreds of thousands, who, otherwise, would wait on our ministry. Slavery, at this moment, is forcing its way over the fairest portions of our country; it is attempting, through the Supreme Court, to nationalize and legalize itself everywhere; it is putting forth strenuous efforts to revive the foreign slave-trade, and also to strike down the liberty of the press and the freedom of the pulpit. The sword is coming upon us, or the 'African flood,' as Bishop Asbury, seventy years ago, denominated the retributive justice of God against slavery. And all the while we are silent—and the silence in many places is deemed a virtue. 'The longer the better.' But is this wise? Is it the more excellent way? Will it lessen the penalty which will surely be executed upon those who oppress the stranger and rob the hireling of his wages?

"With many others, we had supposed that the division of 1844 would have changed our policy on the moral question of slavery. But we have been disappointed. That great disruption was not on moral grounds. The moral question of slavery is yet to be decided."—(*Pamphlet*, p. 7.)

"Few at the East," said the stated clerk of one of the Presbyteries of Illinois to the executive committee of the Home Missionary Society, in 1856, "few at the East, in our Church, are aware of how much we have lost in this State, by our connection with, and support of slavery. Many already have gone, and others are anxious to be out of the connection. Their bond of attachment is greatly weakened for the Church, some of whose members openly practise and boldly justify the system, while others acknowledge its errors, but deny the power or propriety of touching it, and are unwilling that any other body should. The Lord grant you wisdom, grace, and strength to abide by and defend the stand taken." And so it is in our own Church. Thousands turn from us every year, and pass into other churches, who, but for our deep and criminal connection with slavery, would find a home in the Methodist Episcopal Church. But for this huge stumbling-block, we verily believe that from twenty-five to fifty thousand persons who have joined other Churches during the past year (1857–8), would have been to-day on our church records, and numbered with our Israel in the General Minutes. But they will not and cannot join a slaveholding Church. And who can blame them? And what can we say to induce them to do so? Can we deny the fact? Can we justify it? Can we give them any reasonable assurance that it will soon be otherwise? Alas for us as ministers! Alas for Methodism! Alas for Christianity! Take this reproach from us, so that through all New England, and New York, and Pennsylvania, and Ohio, and westward to the Rocky Mountains, we can hold up our heads as Methodist preachers and say, *there is not a slaveholder in the Methodist Episcopal Church—not a bondman owned by a Methodist in all our borders;* and what could we not do, as a Church, by the help of God? If there has been 100,000 increase during the last year, what would it have been if we had been, both in theory and in practice, an anti-slavery Church?

Let us, therefore, rise up and take away this reproach—this rotting putrid carcass, lying at the door of every Methodist Church from the seaboard to Nebraska. Away with it! And let all the people say *Amen!*

VII. *Slaveholding Churches are filling the land with infidelity.* Mistaking Romanism for Christianity, the enlightened portion of the French people turned infidels. If *that* was Christianity, they could not believe in it. And what wonder! So in this country: sensible persons, whose every natural instinct, apart from revelation, teaches them that slaveholding is a great wrong, look on and see Churches making high professions, and speaking great swelling words about *truth*, and *justice*, and *love*, and *purity;* and at the same time not only harboring and tolerating slaveholders in their midst by thousands, and even in the sacred ministry, but *apologizing* for it, and even *defending* it as a Bible institution! What wonder that such things destroy confidence in Christianity! Denounce as loudly as we may the Garrisons, and Fosters, and Phillipses, and Emersons, and Smiths, and Greeleys of the North as "abolitionist skeptics," it was not their abolitionism that made them such. They assailed SLAVERY—"the sum of all villainies"—and found it shielded and defended by Christianity, so called; and they responded, "If this be Christianity, we are not Christians; or at least not of that kind." The rebound from such a contact with a corrupted Church, sent them over to infidelity.

No, gentlemen slaveholders! It was not "abolitionism" that made them skeptical; it was a slaveholding Christianity. Such is always the tendency of corruption in the Church. It was so in England and France two centuries ago, and it is so in the United States to-day. The attitude of the American Churches in regard to SLAVERY,—that parent of every other abomination,—is not only strengthening the hands of infidelity against Christianity in France and England, but in every other nominally Christian country; and especially in these United States. It is sapping the very foundations of all confidence in the Christian religion, in the minds of tens of thousands. Not distinguishing between the loathsome cancer and the rest of the body—between the counterfeit and the genuine,—they condemn the whole, and are thenceforth regarded as infidels. Instead of a slaveholding religion, they accept no religion. And infidelity has no more faithful allies in America, than the D. D.'s and other ministers who defend, or at least apologize for American slavery. They are making more infidels than all the infidel books, and periodicals, and lecturers in the land. Let us then, on this account also—its tendency to infidelity—rise up and put away all slaveholding from the Church of Christ.

VIII. *We have lost enough by slavery already*, and should therefore now get rid of it. In 1843 it drove out some 20,000, more or less, of our best members, in the Northern Conferences, and some 200 ministers. And say what we may, they were noble men. Such were SCOTT, and HORTON, and LEE, and HOES, and SMITH, and PRINDLE, and MATLACK, and others;

noble men—men of principle and conscience—men of intelligence and religion. And the same might be said of thousands among the laity who left us at that time. Many others were "scarcely saved," as FLOY, and TRUE, and NORRIS, and HUESTED, &c., who were well-nigh persecuted out of the Church.

In 1844 slavery wanted a slaveholding bishop; and because it could not be gratified, seceded, and, like the dragon of old, drew the third part of the stars of heaven after it. In this secession we lost some 350,000 members, and about 2000 travelling preachers. Yes, "*lost*," for the Wesleyans in the North are archangels as compared with the slaveholding, women-whipping Methodists of the South. Thus slavery has robbed the Methodist Episcopal Church of near *half a million of her children;* and yet some say, "let it alone—be careful—don't agitate," &c. But we say, *drive it out*, before it corrupts us further, and robs us of thousands more of our legitimate offspring.

IX. *If we do not take some decisive action against it in* 1860, *we are doomed to further secession in the North.* We wish we could believe otherwise. We shall do all we can to prevent it. And yet we do not believe all the bishops, and editors, and preachers in the Methodist Episcopal Church can prevent extensive secessions, both of ministers and members, in 1860, unless something effectual is done at Buffalo for the extirpation of slavery from the Church. Hope has been deferred till the heart is sick. Individuals despaired and left the Church, here and there, on that account, in 1856; and many more would have left, and not a few whole societies, to our personal knowledge, but for the starting of the *Northern Independent*, and the new hope thus begotten, that something effectual will be done in 1860. But let them be disappointed *once more*, and they will leave us forever. The Border know this, and will do all they can to prevent action at Buffalo, and thus to drive many of the best anti-slavery men out of the Church.

We deplore this state of things, but cannot help it. It is *slavery* that produced it; and upon those who plead for slavery in the Church, must all the consequences rest. We say to all abolitionists, STAY IN THE CHURCH! Give no place to the devil. But others are of a different mind. They have been waiting and praying, "O Lord, how long! how long!" till they are gray with years; and they do not wish to take their passports for glory from a Church that holds a hundred thousand slaves! They choose rather to make the painful sacrifice of a separation, and leave their dying testimony against oppression.

Such will leave us by thousands. And when Abel Stevens and others talk so pathetically about "preserving the integrity of the Church," i. e., not taking any action against slavery, lest the Border should carry out their threat and secede, we beg them to remember that the "integrity of the Church" will not be preserved by non-action. We shall do all we can to prevent secession, in such an event, but if no action is had, do what we may, secession will come. We cannot prevent it.

As, therefore, we wish to prevent another secession on our Northern border, and the fires of discord from spreading east, west, and central, we should outlaw slavery in the Methodist Episcopal Church in 1860.

X. *We shall never have any peace in the Church till we put slavery out of it.* And we never ought to have. As in the nation so in the Church—men may think the question is settled, and all will soon be tranquil; but it will never be so till the great *cause* of all our agitations and troubles is put away. In vain shall we pray for the peace of Jerusalem, while slavery reigns within her walls. In vain may we look for concord and harmony, while this apple of discord—this Pandora's box—is in our midst. It is a worse plague to the Church than the Ark of the Lord was to the Philistines. Bring out the new cart, then, and "yoke" thereto, not the slow and patient oxen, but the fleetest horses, and send it back to perdition to return no more.

XI. It is a duty we owe to the slaveholder himself, to settle this question at the earliest possible day. Some of them, like Rev. Mr. Traverse, may not be able to see that it is wrong. They have been so long steeped in it, that they are blinded by it. We ought to let them know, that, in the judgment of the Methodist Episcopal Church, they are sinning against God and their fellow-men; and unless they repent and reform, they can have no more place among us. "Thou shalt in any wise rebuke thy neighbor, and not suffer sin upon sin." It may be, that if thus brought to see their true condition, some of them will repent.

To the same end they should be discarded by all Christians at the North. No slaveholder should ever be admitted into one of our pulpits, come he from whence he may, and be he preacher or bishop. As the English Wesleyans do by such persons, so should we; and then by making the law of the Church to bear specifically upon their great sin, we might renew them again unto repentance, before it is forever too late. At any rate, we ought to do our duty to them, whether they will hear or forbear.

XII. *Finally, we must either extirpate slavery from our midst, or it will ruin the Methodist Episcopal Church.* Already, near 700,000 Methodists are fully sold to this iniquity in the Methodist Episcopal Church South. And in the Northern portion, the Methodist Episcopal Church proper, we have now some 15,000 slaveholders, holding 100,000 slaves; with slaveholding leaders, stewards, trustees, and local preachers, by hundreds, if not by thousands. It has also entered the travelling ministry, and slaveholders are openly tolerated in several of the Conferences, without the slightest disapprobation. Members of our Churches in New York and Philadelphia, if not in Central New York, own slaves in Maryland and Virginia. We have this day (Oct. 20, 1858) received a letter from the West, stating that there is now within the bounds of the Northwest Indiana Conference, a Methodist preacher who says he owns three slaves in Kentucky, and publicly argues that simple slaveholding is not sinful. At a camp-meeting in Central New York, about a year since, we chanced, in the course of a sermon, to utter a few words against slaveholding; whereupon a lady sitting near the stand was very much offended. We learned afterwards that her husband owned some thirty slaves in the South, whose hard toil, no doubt, had furnished the money with which this lady had been so richly attired.

The moral virus is spreading to the very shores of the great lakes. It is corrupting our *literature*, books and periodicals; our *administration;* our *theology;* and our very consciences. The moral sense of the people becomes seared as with a hot iron wherever its withering touch is felt; and it will not remain inactive. Satan was not more dangerous in Paradise, than slavery in a Christian Church. It must either be conquered and exterminated, or it will reign and ruin. It has always been a curse to us; it curses us still; and it will curse us yet more and more till we drive it out of the Church, root and branch. As we love the Church, therefore, and wish either her purity, or peace, or perpetuity, we should outlaw all slaveholding in 1860.

Now let us sum up all these considerations—the fact that slaveholding is a great moral wrong; that our position and practice, in this country, are embarrassing our fellow-laborers in France and England; the noble examples set us by our brethren of other denominations in this country; the noble stand of the American Home Missionary Society; our duty to our common country; the process of emancipation going forward in the Old World; the influence of slavery in repelling men from our communion; the influence of our present position in promoting infidelity; the immense evil slavery has done us already; the certainty of still further trouble if we do not extirpate it; the fact that we can never have any peace while it remains in the Church; that we owe it to the slaveholder himself to deal faithfully with him; and that we must either extirpate slavery or it will utterly corrupt and ruin the Church;—take all these facts into the account, and judge ye, Christian reader, whether we ought to be at ease, and neither say nor do any thing to produce action—*emphatic* and *explicit* ACTION—upon this subject in 1860.

Though generally hopeful and not easily discouraged, we confess to no small degree of sympathy with the correspondent quoted on our title-page—one of the noblest men God has in this lower world—that this will be *among* the last, if not "*the* last opportunity that God's true servants will ever have to restore the Methodist Episcopal Church to her original character, and to preserve her honor in the grandest moral conflict of the age." If we pass 1860, and do nothing, the heart of the Church will fail her, and the hopes of weeping thousands will perish. Our ranks will be broken; some will leave us; others will be discouraged and capitulate; we shall be disgraced, and our honor as a Church trailing in the dust. Slavery and its minions will become more and more imperious; and there will be little to warrant the hope of success for the next twenty years. What we do, therefore, we must make our calculations to do at the next General Conference; for if not done then, it will probably not be done, if ever, till both the writer and reader have passed to the eternal world.

Let it be done then, we say, not in 1864, or 1868, but in 1860! We have no patience with those anti-slavery men, who already begin to say, "If we don't succeed in 1860, we may in 1864." Away with all such tame anti-slavery! "If we don't succeed!" This sing-song of "*next* General Conference," "time enough yet," &c., is the bane of the anti-slavery cause. We say 1860, at all hazards! Let slavery be branded so deeply in the forehead by a clear extirpatory enactment, that the mark shall not be healed till every scar made by its merciless taskmasters, upon the naked quivering flesh of its oppressed millions, shall be healed by the restoring fiat of the resurrection morning!

Christian reader! Will you help us in this patriotic and holy work? Will you *speak*, and *write*, and *vote*, and *give* for your brethren in bonds—for the Church of God which he has purchased with his own blood? Are you in sympathy with this effort? Do you feel for the poor oppressed and bleeding slave? Do you remember him as bound with him?

"Go to the bosom of thy family:
Gather thy little children round thy knees;
Gaze on their innocence, their clear, full eyes,
All fixed on thine, and on their mother; mark
The loveliest look that woman's face can wear,
Her look of love, beholding them and thee;
Then at the altar of your humble joys,
Vow, one by one, vow altogether, vow
With heart and voice, eternal enmity
Against oppression by your brethren's hands;
Till man nor woman, in our wide domain,
Nor son nor daughter, long as time endures,
Shall buy, or sell, or hold, or be a slave."

How this great work is to be accomplished, we will endeavor to show in the next chapter.

CHAPTER X.

HOW SLAVERY CAN BE EXTIRPATED FROM THE METHODIST EPISCOPAL CHURCH.

We have now only to show *how* all slaveholding can be legally excluded from the Methodist Episcopal Church, as proposed in a previous chapter, and our task, so far as this pamphlet is concerned, will be accomplished. We say then—

I. *Let the question of the extirpation of slavery from the Church, be kept distinct from all other questions of Church reform.*

We regard this as a matter of great importance. There are several other questions of reform before the Methodist public: such as lay representation; the extension of the term of ministerial service in the same charge; a modification of the presiding elder's office, &c., with all of which we sympathize personally, and in most of which, we believe, a majority of the laity at least feel a deep interest. And we are ready to do all in our power, in a legitimate and orderly way, to promote the success of each of these reforms. At the same time we say, *keep each movement distinct, and by itself.* There are scores of presiding elders, for instance, who are not in favor of a modification of their office, who will favor extirpation as a distinct question. And so of lay representation, &c. Every such other question that is connected with that of extirpation, will only repel a class of anti-slavery men from this most important of all reforms. We say then, most earnestly, *let the subject of* SLAVERY *stand alone,* and *wholly upon its own merits.* If any wish to petition for lay representation; the extension of the time of ministerial service in the same charge; or a modification of the presiding elder's office; let them do so *in separate petitions:* but let no one of these reforms be encumbered and restricted in their support, by linking it to another movement, which some of its friends cannot help to promote.

II. *Let all that is done be done in the spirit of Christ, and in perfect loyalty to the discipline and government of the Methodist Episcopal Church.*

If we cared nothing for the Church we could go out of her any day, and be free from all further responsibility respecting her complicity with slavery, shaking off the dust of our feet as a testimony against her. But we *love* the Methodist Episcopal Church—her doctrines, and economy, and social means of grace—and are not willing to see her utterly corrupted and ruined by slavery, and consigned to infamy. She is our spiritual mother, and we must not abandon her now that the loathsome virus of slavery has fastened upon her vitals, and threatens to corrupt her very heart's blood. It were ingratitude and cowardice to forsake her now in her extremity. There is balm in Gilead, and a physician there. There *is* hope of her recovery. "Only be strong, and be very courageous." We have no sympathy with despair. We have only to stand firm and do our duty, and the Methodist Episcopal Church may soon be redeemed from her present captivity, and come up out of the wilderness, terrible in moral potency as an army with banners. Her glory *is not* utterly departed. Ichabod *is not* ineffacibly written upon her walls. She *can*, and God helping, *shall* be recovered out of the snare of the devil. The "bushel" of slavery shall not cover her holy candlestick forever. This city of our God, set upon a hill in the sight of all nations a hundred years ago, *shall not* go down into the vale of oppression and moral gloom, to come up no more.

Let every true Methodist, then, stand by and do battle for God and original Methodism. God expects every man to do his duty.. Give no place to the devil. Strike at SLAVERY, but spare Methodism. Slavery is no part of Methodism.

There are those, however, in every Conference, and in almost every society, who, if any thing is said against *slavery* in the Church, and to expose the misconduct of its Methodist apologists and abettors, are ever and anon crying, "Fighting the Church! fighting the Church!" The *effect* of all such sing-song is to *protect slavery* and apologize for it; and the policy is, to throw up "the Church" as a rampart to protect "the sum of all villainies" from the galling fire of *truth*. But let no Methodist be frightened by this pro-slavery bugbear. *Slavery* is not *the Church*. It is because we love the Church and mean to redeem her from impending ruin, that we strike at slavery with the sword of the Lord God. If some timid "anti-slavery men" do cry out "The surgeons are cutting the flesh of our dear mother; do make them desist!" never mind. *Let the cancer come off*, though it may cause some pain, and a little blood may flow. Better these now, than universal corruption and death hereafter. It is a poor kind of filial love that dictates anodynes and delay under such circumstances. But for this healing slightly, our Zion had been completely recovered in 1844, and Heaven forbid that we listen to this moral quackery now, or in 1860. Every one of its advocates, whether aware of it or not, is a foe to the Methodist Episcopal Church, and doing her, so far as his influence goes, the greatest possible injury.

We have said, obey the Discipline and the government of the Church. We mean, the *legitimate* government. But proscription, and persecution, and maladministration, and usurpation, are not the Discipline, nor the government of the Church. To the latter we shall ever bow with implicit obedience; to the former, *never!* "And if that be treason, make the most of it."

III. *We must give no countenance to any attempt to change the Constitution of the Church.*

We have already given reasons why we should attempt nothing of the kind, on page 198; and need not repeat them here. We have little hope in *any thing* but *direct legislation*, by a majority vote, in the chapter on slavery. And time, we believe, will prove to the advocates of a change of the Constitution, that all *such* efforts are worse than useless.

The late Rev. J. V. Watson, editor of the *N. W. C. Advocate*, for a long time clung to the fond hope of changing the Rule, but at length abandoned it altogether; as the following letter, addressed to Rev. Wm. Hosmer, will show:

"Chicago, June 20, 1855.

"Br. Hosmer:—Your paper of late has become of very high practical utility to me. It was always a favorite with a 'but.' I can now dispense with the suffix. Permit me, dear brother, to remind you once again, of the very great desirableness of you and I standing together, upon the subject of direct legislation. If we do not have the satisfaction of *standing* together, we certainly shall have the mortification of *failing* together.

"You will perceive that I have advanced the 'head of my column' right into the field. I am prepared for victory or for death, upon the subject of the change of the chapter. I am not prepared to dole out more 'horse in the mill' arguments to bring about an end which must require *from sixteen to twenty years* to accomplish. In view of the alternate flashing up of the zeal of the progressives, and then again the triumph of the conservatives, I regard a *constitutional change* in the light of an *impracticability*.

"JAMES V. WATSON."

And yet there are professed anti-slavery preachers, and one or two editors in our Church, who are still "doling out" their "horse in the mill" arguments for the change of the Constitution! some because they hope it *may* be accomplished, and others because they *know* it never can.

We stated, on page 99, that even the late Dr. T. E. BOND admitted that the General Conference had a perfect right to legislate slavery out of the Methodist Episcopal Church, by a simple majority vote. We will here give the proof.

In the *Christian Advocate and Journal*, for July 5, 1855, he has an article entitled, "*Prospective action of the General Conference*," in which he says:

"It is, we suppose, settled that the next General Conference cannot alter the General Rule on the subject of slaveholding, by members of the Methodist Episcopal Church, as no proposed amendment of the Rule has received the vote of a constitutional majority of the Annual Conferences to authorize action on the part of the General Conference. *Yet, as the General Conference is competent to pass a simple Rule of Discipline, which will exclude all slaveholders from the Church, without respect to character or circumstances*, the next session of that body will be looked to with more or less apprehension that some Rule will be enacted which will be utterly impracticable in the Conferences having slaveholding territory within their boundaries, and which, from its very introduction into the Discipline, may produce another division of the Church."

By this it appears that the "Old War Horse," as John A. Collins was proud to call him, had never thought of a certain "constitutional" argument, that was presented to the General Conference by a Northern apologist for slavery; nor of the "*ex post facto*" ideas of a few of our Northern preachers. Much as he needed defences for slavery, *he* had never thought of these. We have placed the important passage of the extract in italics, that it may be noticed and pondered. For more of the same character, as touching the question of constitutional slaveholding, see his "*Economy of Methodism*," page 234.

In our opinion, the best course to be taken in the Northern Conferences, when the different propositions for changing the General Rule are presented by the bishops, will be to *lay the whole subject upon the table.* This we have a perfect *right* to do; and however others may think or feel about it, such is, we believe, our safest and best policy. To vote *for* any one of the half dozen schemes that will be presented, will be to enter into Dr. Stevens' diversion policy; to impliedly endorse his doctrine; and to jeopard the Book Room and every church and parsonage in the North, in case the Border secede and sue for the property. And, besides, *it will be of no avail whatever*. Success in that direction is *morally impossible*. On the other hand, to vote *against any* proposition to change the Rule, is to give the enemies of extirpation a pretext for misrepresenting our action, and assailing our sincerity. For these and other reasons we say, lay all such propositions on the table.

As to the "interpretation policy," as it is called (now the favorite policy in the West), we shall vote for it, if it comes before our Conference, though, as already said, we don't like it, and have little confidence in it. The sheet-anchor of our hope is DIRECT LEGISLATION.

IV. *The members of all the anti-slavery Conferences should, at their next sessions, memorialize the General Conference upon the subject.*

These memorials should be uniform, if possible; should pray the General Conference to adopt effectual measures for the extirpation of slavery from the Church, and should be signed by the members of each Conference individually. Very few, even of our most conservative brethren, would refuse to sign such a petition; and such memorials would be vastly more influential with the General Conference than mere resolutions of Annual Conferences. A suitable form of a memorial should be prepared, before the next session of the Baltimore Conference, and measures taken to have a copy presented to the few anti-slavery members of that body; another to those in the Philadelphia Conference; and so on through the East, North, and West. Forty such memorials, signed by four or five thousand Methodist preachers *individually*, would have an overwhelming influence upon the next General Conference. And they might be obtained, and ought to be.

V. *Measures should be taken, in each of the anti-slavery Conferences, at their next session, for the effectual canvassing of every charge within its bounds, for signatures to petitions.*

Petitions were the great lever that moved the British Parliament to emancipate her 800,000 slaves in 1834; and *petitions* will do more than any other single instrumentality in

1860. These petitions should be prepared and sent out under the auspices of the Conferences, and circulated by the preachers. Where the preacher is opposed to the movement, should any such cases be found, some other efficient agency should be employed. The signing should be confined to our membership, and the petitions sent on to the delegates in May, 1860. There should be *half a million of names* to petitions for the disciplinary exclusion of slavery from the Methodist Episcopal Church by the next General Conference. And if we hope for success, we must send in our petitions by thousands, from all parts of the Church. Every charge and appointment should be canvassed. If RICHARD WATSON could lecture on English abolitionism, from place to place, and circulate petitions, as we have shown on page 11, when there was not, in all probability, fifty slaveholders then in all the Wesleyan societies, what ought we to do? If the Wesleyans presented 1958 petitions to Parliament, with 229,426 names attached—1030 petitions and 106,448 more names than were presented by all the other twenty-one dissenting religious bodies in England—what ought we to do, with the slaveholding we now have in the Church, and with our 900,000 members? We have *half a million* of communicants to-day, in the Methodist Episcopal Church, who would sign such a petition if presented to them: and measures ought to be taken by every anti-slavery Conference, at their next session, to canvass every rood of anti-slavery Methodist territory north of the Potomac; and between Massachusetts Bay in the east, and Kansas in the west.

VI. *The more effectually to carry out the preceding measures, and for other purposes, there should be organized, within the bounds of each Annual Conference, a* METHODIST ANTI-SLAVERY UNION.

This is necessary, in order to consolidate the anti-slavery strength of the Church; to produce agreement in sentiment and harmony in action; and to sustain and intensify the anti-slavery sentiment among us, as well as to arrange for and carry out the plan of petitioning. We need something of the kind more fully to enlist our *lay brethren*, who feel as intensely as we ministers do upon the subject; and to give them a chance to share in the responsibility, and labor, and glory of driving slavery out of the Church. We need it, also, to provide means to defray the expenses of circulating documents; the travelling expenses of those whom it may be well to have visit other Conferences, &c. Hitherto one great obstacle to the progress and success of the anti-slavery cause in our Church has been, that it not only had to be carried on by a few preachers, under the frown, if nothing worse, of those in authority, but wholly *at the expense of a few individuals.* Some have sacrificed their earthly all upon this holy altar, and have died poor. Others have given hundreds of dollars, in various ways, and toiled on, amid proscription, and obloquy, and reproach, till they became discouraged, and have given up in despair. We know of one, at least, who has, in various ways, devoted more than $300 during the last three years to this great reform, and will not cease to give so long as he has any thing to employ for such a purpose; but it is not right that the burden should all rest upon a few ministers. All brethren in the ministry who sympathize with the effort should nobly share its sacrifices, as they are, no doubt, willing to do; and the laity, especially, should help to supply "the sinews of war." One hundred thousand copies of pamphlets like McCarter's, and Lame's, and De Vinne's, &c., should be circulated among our people between this and January 1, 1860. Thousands of these should be sent *gratuitously* and post-paid, through the mails. Many of our preachers, even, have not interest enough in the subject to buy any thing of the kind; and if they would, we cannot see them. Our only way, therefore, to get them into their hands, is to send them a copy gratuitously by mail. If thus sent, they would receive and *read* them, and the right effect would be produced. Every travelling preacher, at least, in our Church, should have a copy of some one of these pamphlets, before the session of the Baltimore Conference in March next. The stereotype plates should be paid for, and the pamphlets furnished, as they can be in any quantity, at the *actual cost of manufacturing them.* Anti-slavery men everywhere, preachers and private members, should cast in their offerings into this treasury of the Lord; and help to sustain those who are engaged in this holy warfare, and are perilling almost every thing in the great struggle for the overthrow of slavery in the Methodist Episcopal Church. And we know of no way in which this object can be so effectively aided, as by the organization of Methodist Anti-slavery Unions, by Conferences, and with auxiliaries in the different charges. The auxiliaries, at least, should be composed mainly of laymen, should be as simple as possible in their organization, and confined exclusively to members of our own Church. Such a Union has already been organized within the bounds of the Black River Conference, and has entered upon its labors under the most encouraging auspices. Will not the reader, if an extirpationist, give this subject his immediate attention, and see if he cannot help promote the good cause of purifying and saving the Church, by organizing such a *Union*, either in his Conference, or, if a layman, in the charge where he belongs.* For a printed constitution, and other necessary documents, address, with postage-stamp, Rev. J. C. Vandercook, A. M., Fulton, N. Y.

VII. *Great care should be taken by the anti-slavery men of the Conferences, to send the right kind of delegates to the next General Conference.*

We are aware that this is one of the "delicate questions;" and that whoever shall venture to make the most general suggestion, will be accused of "electioneering," and other kindred offences. Nevertheless, we shall give our opinion.

If any thing is done for the extirpation of the great evil of slavery from the Church, in 1860, we must have delegates who are not only *right in principle*, but who have the *integrity*, and *courage*, and *will*, and *perseverance* to *carry out* their principles. Men who can be bought, or flattered out of their zeal, or intimidated by a frown, or a threat of secession from the Border delegates, are not the men for such a crisis and such a work. It will require MEN. It will require *wisdom* and *grace*, we grant; but there is another quality quite as essential, and perhaps even less common, and that is *stamina;* or what some call "*back-bone*." There are many good, prudent, clever men, who have done good service, and acquired a large influence in their respective Conferences, who, nevertheless, lack this all-important quality. They cower before opposition, and are thrown *hors du combat* by an opinion from a bishop, or a threat of another disruption. They are molluscous in their

* Of course this will not be necessary where efficient Conferences or local Methodist anti-slavery societies exist, and will do the work contemplated by the Union.

mental and moral configuration. Such were the men who were sent reeling by the Episcopal address at the last General Conference. Such were the timid souls (a few only) who, at Indianapolis, declined to sign our protest against Abel Stevens' doctrine, even though the names of such men as HARRIS, and COOKE, and FINLEY, and DEMPSTER, were not withheld for a moment. If Demosthenes could name, as the three main requisites of good oratory, "action! *action!* ACTION!" may we not, with even greater propriety, name, as the qualities most important in a delegate for 1860, "stamina! *stamina!* STAMINA!"

And we must not be misled by professions made in 1859. Look out for sudden conversions. The Malikoff of slavery will not be stormed by new and undisciplined troops. There will be a wonderful screwing up of courage, and a superabundance of anti-slavery sentiment, in certain quarters, in 1859. Men will be "as much opposed to slavery as anybody," will "measure arms with anybody on that subject," will be "out and out anti-slavery," and if they can get upon a committee on slavery, will write and read a magnificent report for their respective Conferences. We have seen this game played over and over again; and have often seen it so successful with the younger members of the Conferences, as to prevent the election of some of the very best candidates.

Barnum has an *aquarium* in his museum in New York. Its sides are of glass, and it is so placed that when a fish sails up towards the top of the water, he is between the beholder and a strong light. Under these circumstances, the *flesh* of the fish's body being semi-transparent, his spine, or back-bone, can be distinctly traced from one end to the other. Indeed, he looks more like a skeleton fish than a living one. Now we have a few candidates for honors, in all the Conferences, who keep down at the bottom of the ecclesiastical aquarium for three sessions out of four, swimming around among the sea-weed and sediment of "prudence," and "moderation," and "loyalty," and the "mere question of means," &c., but once in four years they sail up most gracefully into the light, and exhibit their spinal column. "Just see what a back-bone I've got! Don't you see it in my *report?* Didn't you see it in my *speech?* Don't you see how I *vote* on all the anti-slavery resolutions?" And the moment the election is over, down they go again to the bottom, and we hear no more of their anti-slavery views for the next four years.

Now *such* men (and we have no individual in our eye, and call no names), but *such* men, however dignified, or honored, or wise, or prudent, are not the men to legislate slavery out of the Methodist Episcopal Church in 1860.

Another suggestion: No man should be proscribed for his *office*, or relation to the Church, as an editor, or teacher, or presiding elder. And yet, as the executive government of the Church is clearly opposed to such legislation, it is quite natural that all the official appointees of that government should be at least very conservative. Such is the case with a large majority of our presiding elders. But there are many honorable exceptions, and *such* should not be proscribed for their office' sake. Still, it is a melancholy fact, not only that 97 out of 221 delegates in the last General Conference were presiding elders, but that a very large majority of them voted against nearly every measure of reform. Unless, therefore, such men are known to maintain a good profession, despite the tendency of their office to tone down their anti-slavery, they are not the right kind of men to send to Buffalo. And 97 presiding elders, to 124 regular preachers (minus a score or so of teachers, agents, editors, &c.), is too large a proportion from one class in the ministry. One from each Conference, making about twenty-five per cent. of the whole, is abundantly a sufficient number of presiding elders. And let them be true and tried men, or else don't send them. Above all, we should be careful and not send men who, in the heat of battle, will lose sight of the enemy, and turn and bayonet their fellow-soldiers.

VIII. *A chapter on slavery should be prepared, and, as far as possible, agreed upon by the principal anti-slavery men in the Northern Conferences, before the meeting of the Annual Conferences next year.*

The *policy* of direct legislation, and, if possible, a draft of a law, embodying the two principles of prohibition and extirpation, should be made the test of legislative orthodoxy in 1859. We want some line to work to. If all is left unsettled, the delegates will be in confusion when they reach Buffalo, some with this scheme and some with that, and, as in 1856, nothing will be done. The getting up of this preliminary outline of a chapter on slavery, is, in our view, one of the most important subjects to which the various committees of correspondence can now direct their attention. They should have the results of their correspondence and labors ready to present to each of the Conferences at their next sessions, and before the election of delegates. The Black River Committee are ready at all times to co-operate with other similar committees, in consummating such an arrangement.

IX. The delegates having been elected, it might be well to have *a convention of all those in favor of direct extirpatory legislation*, to meet some time in the fall or winter of 1859–60. Or, if this were thought too expensive, a meeting of one man from each delegation might answer the same purpose. In this meeting the chapter should be matured, and arrangements made to guard against defeat, and secure success.

X. *A strong body of anti-slavery laymen should attend the next General Conference.*

Slavery has always exerted great influence over the General Conference by her lobby. Slaveholders visited Indianapolis in troops, in May, 1856. They did all they could to get the *time* of holding the General Conference changed, so that it should not come on the year of the presidential election; and then to get the *place* of our next session fixed for Baltimore, instead of Buffalo. Thank God, it is on *free soil.* The everlasting thunder of old Niagara may help to peal the death-knell of slavery. Our border will be *free Canada*, instead of slavebreeding Virginia or Carolina. Let the sturdy laymen of our Northern Conferences provide for the necessary labor on the farms, and come up to Buffalo by hundreds. Every public house in the city ought to be filled with them. The great question of their admission to the Annual and General Conferences is to be debated and settled there; and the still greater question, of slavery or no slavery in the Methodist Episcopal Church. Let the laity, then, form a solid rampart, a National Guard, behind the ministry, in this last, and desperate, and yet victorious struggle against the abomination that maketh desolate. It is the last time, we hope, that the laity of our Church will ever attend either an Annual or a General Conference, without a disciplinary representation in all our councils.

X. *Timely precaution should be taken to have the proceedings of the General Conference properly reported, and impartially published.*

We have no disposition to censure any who had to do with these matters at the last General Conference, and yet certain things transpired there, in regard to reporting and printing, that ought not to occur again. For instance, on the 22d day of May, 1856, on motion of the writer, the General Conference ordered 5000 copies of the majority and minority reports on slavery, to be published in pamphlet form, for the use of that body, the design being, as stated at the time, to send them to our constituencies in the several Conferences. But instead of obeying this order of the General Conference, the Agents (under whose advice we will not say) took the responsibility of neglecting to print the reports; and to this day they have never seen daylight, except in the columns of that ephemeral sheet, the *Daily Western Christian Advocate.* They were not even published in the printed journal. All we have on record concerning the character of these two important reports, is contained in these four lines: "Mr. Raymond, chairman of the Committee on Slavery, presented a report, proposing changes in the Discipline on the subject of slavery. It lies over under the rule, and on motion was ordered to be printed." Now why did not these reports appear, as ordered? and who suppressed them? And so of Brother DENNIS's speech on the election of the editor of the *N. C. Advocate.* Why was *that* suppressed? And if we should have reporters and publishers in 1860, who take the liberty to assort and sift out matters to suit *their* notions of propriety, how much of fair play will there be for the anti-slavery cause? And what will the public know hereafter of the actual proceedings? A crisis is upon the Church. 1860 will be an epoch in her history, and the doings of that General Conference should be faithfully and fairly reported, and fully and honestly printed. It is due to Methodism and to impartial history. And if the anti-slavery men of the body wish justice done to them before the public, and by the future historian, they should see to it in time, that the system of garbling and blanketing, so successfully practised at Indianapolis in 1856, should not bear sway again in Buffalo in 1860.

XI. *Petitions, or a deputation, should be sent to both the British Wesleyan and the Canada Conferences, at their next sessions, informing them of the true state of things in the Methodist Episcopal Church, in regard to slavery, and entreating them, for the love of Christ, to renew their former noble testimony against it, in our next General Conference.*

Formerly the delegates from the British Conference especially bore testimony, either in the addresses they brought, or in their oral communications to the General Conference, against the sin of slaveholding. The last of these testimonies, we believe, was in their address to the General Conference of 1844. Previously to that, they had been even more earnest and explicit. In 1848, Dr. DIXON bore a brief letter of introduction, in which nothing was said about slavery; and he said nothing against its morality, or its continuance, in his oral addresses. In 1852 no delegate was sent to us, and the address, sent by mail, failed to reach the General Conference. What it contained is not therefore known. In 1856 Dr. HANNAH brought a brief address, silent upon the subject of slavery, and both he and Mr. JOBSON maintained the most studied silence upon the subject in all their public addresses. The same, we believe, has been true of the deputations from Canada, for several sessions past.

Now we should entreat our elder brethren, both in England and in Canada, not to leave us thus involved in slavery, without their continued and fraternal admonitions, line upon line, precept upon precept. Shall the Protestant Churches of France plead with the American Churches to free themselves from slavery, and the British Wesleyan Conference cease to entreat her children in this New World, who are now more deeply involved in slavery, in all probability, than any other Church in the land?

Our brethren in England do not know the truth in regard to our connection with slavery, or they would certainly renew their former testimony against it, if they did not actually decline all fraternal relation with us; and we should take measures to put them in possession of the truth, and entreat them to do their duty to the Methodist Episcopal Church in America. And so of the Canada Conference. If both these were to urge their remonstrances upon the attention of the next General Conference, it would greatly encourage the enemies of slavery, and promote the great object we ardently hope to see accomplished.

XII. We venture another suggestion. The usual course at General Conference has been to have a committee on slavery, to whom all petitions and memorials were referred. For this purpose, such a committee may be well enough, but we have not the highest confidence in its utility, as a means of promoting extirpatory legislation. It is more likely to tone down and take the stamina out of some ten or twenty anti-slavery men, and to get them into a tissue of miserable compromises, than to report any thing worthy of the anti-slavery struggle. In 1852 they did not report at all. It was a great cistern in which to strangle anti-slavery petitions and resolutions, and to drown earnest anti-slavery men. In 1856 it served to stave off all action for weeks, and when at last the report came in, the very concessions and compromises agreed to by the anti-slavery portion of the committee, in hope that the Border would then go with them, were seized upon and ridiculed, by the Border delegates, as gross inconsistencies. So that, as a whole, the committee on slavery in the General Conference have not greatly served the cause of anti-slavery for several sessions past. And we have but little to hope from them in future. Still, one will no doubt be ordered, and it will hang from week to week, as usual, without reporting. The pro-slavery members of it can always stave off action in committee for some time, and afterwards in the Conference, till towards the close of the session; and *then* appropriate discussion and action will be next to impossible.

Our plan would be, therefore, to have a chapter prepared, as suggested on a previous page, and presented to the General Conference *early in the session;* and then, if the committee do not report a suitable bill during the *second week of the session*, to take up the chapter, and press it to a vote; voting down all postponements, amendments, divisions, riders, and extinguishers whatsoever. We see no other way that any thing can ever be accomplished. If this great question is allowed to lie over till the third week of the session, either to wait for the committee to report, or from any other considerations, *we are again defeated!* Other matters will first be pressed with unyielding tenacity for three or four days; then a motion will be made and carried, that, "as there is so much important business to be done, the bishops select and bring forward such business as *they* think most important" (and they will never call up the subject of slavery), and thus the whole thing will be again strangled.

Our only hope of appropriate action at all, so far as past experience may be our guide, is in *early* action; and the only certain way to secure early action, is to be prepared to bring up the subject in due time and form (if the committee do not report in season, or if they report another compromise bill), and press it to a vote. The policy of the slave interest always has been, and still will be, to *stave off action*, to allow them time to concert measures to distract and divide us, and to intimidate, and buy, and flatter such as can be thus influenced, into their "peace and quiet" measures.

XIII. *Finally, we must not fail to lean upon God for wisdom and strength in this great struggle.*

It was only when Moses' hands were raised in prayer that Israel prevailed. We shall have much to try our courage, and fortitude, and patience, and charity. The battle with slavery, even in the Church, is not to be fought without wounds, and blood, and scars. But let us be patient, though deliberate and determined. The weapons of our warfare are not carnal, but spiritual. While we never muffle the edge of the sword, nor swathe it in the silken folds of a temporizing expedience, let us so live as at all times to be able to cry, "the sword of THE LORD and of Gideon." Let us hold on to God. We have none of us any thing to gain, but as we gain it through a purified Church and holier life—greater usefulness and success in the Church on earth, and brighter glory in heaven.

The CHURCH! Mark ye well her bulwarks! Consider her palaces! And who will not say, "If I forget thee, O Jerusalem, let my right hand forget her cunning! Let my tongue cleave to the roof of my mouth, if I prefer not Jerusalem above my chief joy!" It is *because* we love the Church, and mean to live, and labor, and die in her, that we are impelled to toil, and sacrifice, and suffer, if need be, for her honor, and purity, and peace.

"For her our tears shall fall;
For her our prayers ascend;
To her our cares and toils be given,
Till toils and cares shall end."

And if any of us, in our efforts to deliver our beloved Zion from the withering scourge of slavery, should degenerate in personal piety, and lose in any measure the spirit of Christ, it would be to us a costly warfare. May the Lord breathe upon us the Holy Ghost, that if reviled we may suffer it, and still love and pray for those who persecute or despitefully use us.

But still, *we must not cease to agitate*, and *must not withhold the truth* from the people, let it cut where it may. A want of knowledge as to the connection of our Church with slavery, has been one of the chief causes of our present deep corruption; and a knowledge of the truth among the people generally, is now essential to appropriate interest and action, and our purification and recovery.

Our task is now done. We have sketched our history, from a pure anti-slavery Church, to a deeply corrupted and practically pro-slavery one—have shown our present deplorable condition, and its remedy—have shown *why* that remedy should be applied, and *how* the desired purification may be realized. We shall endeavor, as God may grant us life, and health, and wisdom, and grace, and means, to carry out the measures we have indicated. It remains for the reader to determine, whether or not *he* will also do his part. We write and stereotype these pages at our own cost, to the amount of over a hundred dollars before the first sheet can be printed, without ever expecting to realize one dollar out of five in return. But we do it for God, and for our bleeding and dishonored Zion, appealing to the ETERNAL JUDGE for the purity of our motives, the sincerity of our sympathy with the oppressed, and our final reward.

If the reader is a Methodist—so far at least as slavery is concerned, an "old-fashioned Methodist"—and really desires to see this great question settled, so far as the Methodist Episcopal Church is concerned, at the next General Conference, give to this extirpation movement your hearty and unwavering support. Sustain those periodicals that are doing most to promote this object. Encourage your minister to agitate the subject in his charge; to preach upon it; and to circulate petitions. Take hold of the matter yourself, and work in good earnest till the glorious victory is achieved. May the Lord grant us all needful wisdom, and grace to do *our whole duty*, in this great moral exigency; and, when the Chief Shepherd shall appear, crown us with his faithful and ransomed hosts, with everlasting life. *Amen.*

NOTE.—One most excellent method of promoting the anti-slavery cause in the Church, is by the circulation of pamphlets. No one can tell how much good a single dollar, expended in this way, will be likely to do. We have the excellent pamphlets of Brothers McCARTER and LAME, of the Philadelphia Conference, and also our own; any or all of which we will send in bundles, by express, to any part of the country, at *the actual cost of manufacturing;* that is, *without a farthing of profit.* We want none. Our sole aim is to scatter *truth.* Could not the reader get up a *Union*, or a subscription, and send on from five to ten dollars for a supply of these pamphlets? One should be put into every Methodist family in the land.

We state no price, but simply say, that for such distribution, or for sale again, we will supply this pamphlet, or either of the others named, at *actual cost.*

Direct letters to the Author, care of Messrs. Mason Brothers, New York.

www.ingramcontent.com/pod-product-compliance
Lightning Source LLC
LaVergne TN
LVHW021416110826
845150LV00007B/1950

* 9 7 8 1 4 2 5 5 0 9 7 3 6 *